Officer Survival

Training Scenarios

Scott Kirshner

Neither the author nor the publisher assumes any responsibility for the

use or misuse of information contained in this book.

<u>DEDICATION</u>

This book is dedicated to those officers who have perished in the line of duty and to those who have been seriously injured protecting the community.

Your sacrifice will never be forgotten.

It is also dedicated to all training officers who spend countless hours writing training curriculum and facilitating classes. It is a worthy and noble endeavor.

Table of Contents

Scott Kirshner

ACKNOWLEDGMENTS

I would like to acknowledge all those who have been involved in my training and growth as an instructor. Along the journey there have been many people who have influenced me. Sometimes I learn improved ways to teach a skill or facilitate an important topic while other times I learn what not to do which is equally important. All of these experiences have made me a better instructor.

Many valuable lessons have been learned and shared.

Scott Kirshner

Introduction

Over the years I have spoken with literally thousands of probation and parole officers regarding officer safety and survival. The one common theme for many community corrections officers is the lack of realistic, ongoing, and practical officer survival training. Very few departments engage in scenario based training, stress inoculation training or reality based training. While some departments provide exceptional training with annual training requirements this seems to be the exception and not the rule. My impression is that many departments do the bare minimum when it comes to officer survival training. This has been expressed to me time and time again. This is a disservice to officers who supervise individuals who possess a propensity to violate the law. Some officers have expressed that the only safety training they received was verbal de-escalation while others say they had OC training once. Typically, the training is a one-time event and there is no follow up training. This lack of training is far from adequate to prepare officers who may one day find themselves in a violent encounter against a dedicated threat.

> A "**Dedicated Threat**" is a person or persons whose main goal, desire, and motivation is to severely injure or kill you by any means necessary.

The goal of this book is to provide training officers and front line officers scenarios that can be used either individually by an officer or, more preferably, in a training environment. The following scenarios can also be used and discussed as part of a unit meeting. Unfortunately, there is such a lack of consistency between different probation and parole departments that it is very likely you will need to modify the scenarios to fit the policy and procedure of your department. Additionally, the scenarios may need to be modified based upon the type of officer safety equipment that you are issued. Some departments do not issue any equipment while others provide only OC spray. And then there are departments who issue handcuffs, OC spray, batons, Taser's, and handguns. Some departments are even issuing rifles to their Fugitive Apprehension Units. A few departments are progressive while others are years behind the times when it comes to officer safety and survival. Only you will know where your department stands in relation to your officer survival training, equipment and policy. Therefore, modify the scenarios to fit your needs. Ultimately, you want to develop the ability to respond to violence within the confines of law, judicial code, and department policy. On top of this you need to respond based upon the safety equipment that you are issued – if any! This means that you may be severely restricted if you do not have any safety equipment or you might have many options if you are issued a variety of safety equipment. When reviewing a scenario feel free to modify factors such as:

- Safety equipment that you are carrying

- Potential malfunction of safety equipment

- Ineffectiveness of safety equipment

- Whether you are working with a partner(s)

- Injury that you or your partner receives

- Gender of the offender

- Age of the offender

- Number of offenders

- Physical fitness/health status of offender

- Type of weapon that the offender possesses

- Proximity of offender

- Time of the day

- Environmental factors

- Lighting factors

- Location of incident

- Escape routes

Officer Survival Training Scenarios

Keep in mind that a small modification to a scenario can completely change the dynamics of the response. It is a worthy endeavor to practice different versions of a scenario to see how it could potentially change the way the officer responds to the encounter. If you are reviewing the scenarios in a group setting such as a unit meeting it is important to note that different officers may respond differently to the same set of factors. A petite female officer may respond differently than a large physically fit male officer. In such situations it is worthy to discuss such factors so that the group understands how different factors and dynamics impact a use of force response. Your ability to verbalize and document this information is critical.

The presented scenarios are not provided in any particular order. The main reason for this is so that no discernable pattern is presented and so that you respond solely based on the presented information taking into account any modifications that you include in the scenario. Do not make any assumptions that scenarios are presented from the lowest level of force to the highest level of force. The real world does not work that way so there is no benefit in having the scenarios in a particular order. Therefore, all scenarios are random and should be handled based on the scenario and not the order that the scenario is placed within the book. Regardless of how you conduct the scenario whether individually, group environment or a hands on training scenario it is absolutely critical that you understand no scenario is designed to be a "no-win" situation. And, officers should never be made to intentionally fail a scenario. This will only damage the officer's confidence and motivation to train. The objective is that the officer never gives up and always wins. This does not mean that the scenario will not be difficult or challenging. Officers that make mistakes in training must learn from such mistakes in a positive manner that encourages learning. They must also build upon their success with more challenging scenarios.

It is highly recommended for that each scenario you complete you also write a use of force report that clearly, accurately, and factually documents the reasoning for your chosen level of force. While this may not be an enjoyable task you can think of it as defensive tactics report writing which can save you from liability after a use of force incident. The only way you will get better at writing use of force reports is by practicing writing use of force reports. There is no shortcut to this process. Keep in mind that your documentation may be scrutinized word for word in a courtroom one day. An attorney may look to twist your words around so it is critical to write a clear and accurate report. Again, because there is such a wide variance in the format of reports between departments I highly encourage you to use the exact format that your department utilizes. While this is time consuming it will also provide you with valuable experience and practice writing use of force reports. These are the same reports that will be used in court, often years later, to defend your actions should you be sued. Your memory of the event may change over time but your use of force report will be the same as the day you wrote it. It is also important to be familiar with the U.S. Supreme Court case Graham v. Connor.

Graham v. Connor, 490 U.S. 386, 396-97 (1989)

When it comes to use of force, specifically excessive force, the landmark case is Graham v. Conner which is the national standard that is utilized today. In this 1989 case the U.S. Supreme Court declared use of force to be a Fourth Amendment issue subject to an "*objective reasonableness*" standard.

The ruling states the following:

- The "reasonableness" of a particular use of force must be judged from the perspective of a reasonable officer on the scene, rather than the 20/20 vision of hindsight.

- The calculus of reasonableness must embody allowance for the fact that police officers are often forced to make split-second judgments – in circumstances that are tense, uncertain, and rapidly evolving – about the amount of force that is necessary in a particular situation.

- The "reasonableness" inquiry in an excessive force case is an objective one: the question is whether the officers' actions are "*objectively reasonable*" in light of the facts and circumstances confronting them, without regard to their underlying intent or motivation.

Based on this information, when attempting to determine the reasonableness of an officer's use of force it must be done under the following conditions:

1. Judge through the perspective of a "reasonable officer at the scene".

    This reasonable officer is expected to view the incident based upon similar circumstances and with the same or similar training and experience.

2. Judgment must be based upon the totality of the facts known to the officer at the time the force was applied.

    One cannot use hindsight or base judgment on information that is found *after* the conclusion of the incident.

3. Based on the facts known to the officer without regard to the underlying intent or motivation.

    What was the information the officer had that lead to his/her decision to use a particular level of force?

The proper application of what is reasonable takes into account the facts and circumstances of each particular case to include:

-   The severity of the crime

-   Whether the suspect poses an immediate threat to the safety of the officers or others

-   Whether the suspect is actively resisting arrest or attempting to evade arrest by flight

- The fact that officers are often required to make split-second judgments

It is important for officers to understand the standards that Graham establishes. For example, an officer's use of force that ends up in litigation may end up being resolved in the safety and comfort of a courtroom many years after the incident. An attorney may try to present information to a jury that was not known to the officer at the time that force was used against an offender. It is easy to look back in time with "*hindsight bias*" and state that the officer 'should have' or 'could have' done this or that. Such a maneuver is not right or fair to the officer. Fortunately, Graham does not allow this to happen. Additionally, each particular case is judged on the facts and circumstances of the incident. Information that was not known to the officer cannot be used against an officer after the fact.

> **"H*indsight Bias*" is not beneficial to the officer and is not allowed per Graham v. Connor.**

Being that such litigation often happens years after the incident it is imperative that officers write a well written use of force report that accurately and factually explains exactly why the officer used force and that the level of force used was reasonable based on the offenders/subjects actions. Your ability to write an excellent use of force report may benefit you years down the line after the original incident.

Graham v. Connor

The Supreme Court of the United States regarding use of force:

- Objective Reasonableness

- Based on Totality of Circumstances

- The calculus of reasonableness must embody allowance for the fact that police officers are often forced to make split-second judgments – in circumstances that are tense, uncertain, and rapidly evolving – about the amount of force that is necessary in a particular situation.

- The "reasonableness" of a particular use of force must be judged from the perspective of a reasonable officer on the scene, rather than with 20/20 vision of hindsight.

- The test of reasonableness under the Fourth Amendment is not capable of precise definition or mechanical application.

- Its proper application requires careful attention to the facts and circumstances of each particular case, including the severity of the crime at issue, whether the suspect poses an immediate threat to the safety of the officers or others, and whether he is actively resisting arrest or attempting to evade arrest by flight.

Graham clearly states that use of force will be impacted by the ***totality of circumstances*** so it is important that either individually or as a group you determine what factors or variables influence your force decision.

Such variables may include the following:

Subject:

- Physical size of subject
- Mental state of subject
- Skill level
- Demeanor
- Weapons
- Under the influence of drugs or alcohol
- Other

Officer:

- Experience
- Level of training
- Physical size
- Injury to officer or exhaustion due to a physical confrontation
- Other

Environmental:

- Innocent bystanders
- Crowded location
- Location – isolated, rural environment, urban environment
- Night time – low light, no light conditions
- Extreme heat or cold conditions
- Rain, snow, wet or slippery ground
- Road hazards

<u>Other Variables or Factors:</u>   •

- Number of subjects
- Is the subject resisting?
- Is the subject fleeing?
- Is the subject's actions *not likely* to cause death or serious bodily injury?
- Is the subject's actions *likely* to cause death or serious bodily injury?
- Proximity of police assistance/response time

Media Bias and Social Media

Writing an effective Use of Force Incident Report is also important, in part, due to the mostly negative impact of media bias and social media. Today, everyone has a cellphone with the ability to video an incident. Within minutes of an incident occurring you can become an instant internet sensation and not in a positive manner. Within hours your use of force incident may be shown on news channels across the world. And make no mistake –

YOUR ACTIONS WILL BE JUDGED BY THE COURT OF POPULAR OPINION

We live in a world where everyone on the internet thinks that they are a use of force subject matter expert (SME). The same goes for the media which often intentionally show a story in a bias fashion and then provides commentary that is either totally incorrect or inflammatory. And, there is a very strong likelihood that it is based on incomplete information. Anti-law enforcement bias is currently rampant in the United States and the media is adding fuel to the fire. And, just because you work in community corrections as a parole officer or a probation officer you ARE included under the law enforcement umbrella. Do not expect any special privileges from the media or the community that you are attempting to keep safe. Yes, there are bad law enforcement officers who must be dealt with appropriately. Yes, there are officers who make bad decisions who must be held accountable for their actions. Law enforcement officers who behave unethically or act inappropriately taint all the officers who conduct themselves appropriately. In general, the vast majority of law enforcement officers whether police, probation, parole, corrections, or detention work both morally and ethically. These officer take their job duties seriously and believe in the oath that they have sworn to uphold. All officers should not be blanketed with shame and bias based on the actions of a few bad officers. Media bias is a reality that cannot be ignored or minimized.

An excellent example of media bias was the shooting of Michael Brown by Police Officer Darren Wilson of the Ferguson Police Department. The whole *"Hands Up; Don't Shoot"* was a blatant lie that was proven to be false but this did not prevent the media from continuing to report on it, television shows who put it in their storyline, daytime talk show hosts who provided false information, professional athletes who perpetuated the false narrative, and even politicians who gave speeches based on this lie. According to the **Department of Justice Report Regarding the Criminal Investigation into the Shooting Death of Michael Brown By Ferguson, Missouri Police Officer Darren Wilson**[i] dated March 4, 2015:

"Although there are several individuals who have stated that Brown held his hands up in an unambiguous sign of surrender prior to Wilson shooting him dead, their accounts do not support a prosecution of Wilson. As detailed throughout this report, some of those accounts are inaccurate because they are inconsistent with the physical and forensic evidence; some of those accounts are materially inconsistent with that witness's own prior statements with no explanation, credible or otherwise, as to why those accounts changed over time. Certain other witnesses who originally stated Brown had his hands up in surrender recanted their original accounts, admitting that they did not witness the shooting or parts of it, despite what they initially reported either to federal or local law enforcement or to the media. Prosecutors did not rely on those accounts when making a prosecutive decision."

The Department of Justice report states:[ii]

> *"Based on this investigation, the Department has concluded that Darren*
>
> *Wilson's actions do not constitute prosecutable violations under the*
>
> *applicable federal criminal civil rights statute, 18 U.S.C. § 242, which*
>
> *prohibits uses of deadly force that are "objectively unreasonable," as*
>
> *defined by the United States Supreme Court. The evidence, when viewed*
>
> *as a whole, does not support the conclusion that Wilson's uses of deadly*
>
> *force were "objectively unreasonable" under the Supreme Court's definition.*
>
> *Accordingly, under the governing federal law and relevant standards set*
>
> *forth in the USAM, it is not appropriate to present this matter to a federal*
>
> *grand jury for indictment, and it should therefore be closed without*
>
> *prosecution."*

As indicated in the last paragraph it is clear that the U.S. Supreme Court Case in Graham v. Connor, 490 U.S. 386, 396-97 (1989) is referenced in this DOJ report. The bottom line was that Police Officer Darren Wilson was JUSTIFIED in his use of force in the killing of Michael Brown. How often did you hear the media, politicians, activists, residents of Ferguson, daytime television hosts, professional athletes, etc. apologize to Officer Wilson for doing his job?

It is also important to note that according to the DOJ report:[iii]

> *"The encounter between Wilson and Brown took place over an*
>
> *approximately two-minute period of time at about noon on August 9, 2014."*

Two minutes is not a lot of time and you can see how fast events can turn violent and deadly. This is important to consider when conducting the scenarios in this book. You will have time to think, evaluate, and postulate on the presented scenario under no stress or pressure of injury. But, in a real world situation you will not have this luxury.

This is why realistic and ongoing training is critically important. You must be able to accurately perceive the situation and then determine an appropriate course of action. You need to be able to do this under pressure and in a rapid manner of time. Under the best of circumstances this is asking a lot of anyone. Training should never be considered a luxury. Regular, practical and realistic training is a must. And even when you do everything correctly there will be internet keyboard warriors and bias media who will prosecute you unjustly in the court of popular opinion! Welcome to the new reality. The media rarely has all the facts of a use of force incident but this will not prevent them from speculating or reporting part of the story.

Regarding the Michael Brown incident how often did you hear the media report the following which was documented in the DOJ report:[iv]

> *"Brown and Witness 101 had just come from Ferguson Market and Liquor ("Ferguson Market"), a nearby convenience store, where, at approximately 11:53 a.m., Brown stole several packages of cigarillos. As captured on the store's surveillance video, when the store clerk tried to stop Brown, Brown used his physical size to stand over him and forcefully shove him away."*

Often, Brown was made out to be an innocent young boy. Clearly, this was not the case. The media almost exclusively focused on the actions of Officer Wilson and dismissed the actions of Brown. The media ran with eyewitness statements which were not credible yet were told repeatedly further perpetuating a false narrative that the public held onto and believed. Officer Wilson was crucified unjustly by the news media and social media such as Facebook, Twitter and others. This is unacceptable and should never be the case. The media failed Officer Darren Wilson and many on social media continually perpetuated the lies. Many of these lies and false statements are still believed today by residents of Ferguson despite the DOJ report.

The DOJ report states:

> *"The media has widely reported that there is witness testimony that Brown said "don't shoot" as he held his hands above his head. In fact, our*

investigation did not reveal any eyewitness who stated that Brown said "don't shoot."

It is important to reiterate that the slogan, *"Hands up; don't shoot"* was a complete lie! But, that did not stop it from being repeatedly and falsely sold. Such lies only help feed anti-law enforcement sentiment and racial divisiveness.

Again, according to the DOJ report:[v]

> *"There are no credible witness accounts that state that Brown was clearly attempting to surrender when Wilson shot him. As detailed throughout this report, those witnesses who say so have given accounts that could not be relied upon in a prosecution because they are irreconcilable with the physical evidence, inconsistent with the credible accounts of other eyewitnesses, inconsistent with the witness's own prior statements, or in some instances, because the witnesses have acknowledged that their initial accounts were untrue.*
>
> *ii. Wilson Did Not Willfully Violate Brown's Constitutional Right to Free from Unreasonable Force"*

The bottom line is that Police Officer Darren Wilson's actions were justified and he did not violate Michael Brown's constitutional rights.

This is not to state that Ferguson Police Department does not have valid problems that need to be properly addressed. The focus in this section was strictly on the use of force by Officer Darren Wilson and is not to imply that other problems do not exist within the Ferguson Police Department. Those are separate issues from the focus of this book. To understand the other issues you can refer to the **Investigation of the Ferguson Police Department, United States Department of Justice Civil Rights Division**[vi] dated March 4, 2015. It is apparent that the Ferguson Police Department does have numerous problems that need to be remedied.

Scenario Format

Each scenario starts out with a brief description of the scenario. Remember, you can modify the scenario to fit your needs. You can choose what safety equipment you are carrying or not carrying, the location, time of day, number of offenders, lighting conditions, size of the subject, special skills that the subject may possess, etc. You have complete creative control. I also recommend making slight modifications to the scenario to see if or how it will change your response. After the description you will have the elements of force: Ability, Opportunity, Jeopardy, and Preclusion. This is a process that will allow you to cognitively work through the scenario in a logical manner and then determine the appropriate response.

Elements of Force:

Ability - an attacker possesses the power to injure or kill. This power may come in the form of a weapon (gun, knife, club, etc.) or through disparity of force.

- ♦ Does the subject have <u>ability</u> to do harm to you as the officer or to a third party?

    ___ Yes   ___ No

Opportunity - an attacker is capable of immediately employing the power to injure or kill. Two components to opportunity are distance and obstacles.

- ♦ Does the subject have <u>opportunity</u> to do harm to you as the officer or to a third party?

    ___ Yes   ___ No

Jeopardy - an attacker is acting in such a manner that a reasonable and prudent person would conclude he/she intends to injure or kill.

- ◆ Are you or a third party in jeopardy?   ____ Yes   ____ No

Preclusion - officer assessment to determine if a lower level of force would be appropriate or ineffective; and retreat is not possible.

What level of force is appropriate?

- ◆ Is retreat possible?   ____ Yes   ____ No

Elements of Force in More Detail

Use of force policies will often discuss "Elements of Force" pertaining to when an officer is justified in using force.

Elements of force include:

Ability: An attacker possesses the power to injure or kill.
This power may come in the form of a **weapon** or through **disparity of force**.

Utilization of a weapon by an attacker clearly gives that person an advantage. Even items not designed as weapons can cause lethal injuries such as a baseball bat, screwdriver, tire iron and even rope.

Weapon:
- ▪ Gun
- ▪ Knife
- ▪ Sword
- ▪ Club
- ▪ Tire iron
- ▪ Baseball bat

Disparity of Force: Is a situation which places you at an overwhelming disadvantage in your effort to protect yourself against immediate and serious bodily injury.

Factors include:

- Age: Offender is 22 years old and the officer is 55 years old

- Size: Offender is a 6'2" tall male; officer is a 5'8" male

- Strength: Offender is a muscular bodybuilder

- Gender: Offender is large, in shape male; officer is a petite female

- Numbers: You are outnumbered; 2+ attackers verse you

- Skill Level: The offender is a martial artist, boxer, weapons expert, etc.

Opportunity: An attacker is capable of immediately employing the power to injure or kill.

An attacker needs more than just the ability to injure or kill you they need the opportunity to cause you harm immediately as in right here and right now. Realistically there are many people with the ability to hurt, injure, maim, and kill you but they do not have the opportunity because they are not near you to inflict harm. Two components to opportunity are distance and obstacles.

Distance:

The attacker needs to be close enough to you to actually be a threat. This can be dependent on the type of weapon used. An attacker with a baseball bat who is 50 yards from you is not much of a threat. An attacker holding a knife who is 30 feet from you may be considered a lethal situation. An attacker holding a handgun who is 10 yards from you may be considered a lethal situation. An attacker holding a tire iron and cursing at you from across a busy parking lot is probably not a much of a threat.

Obstacles:

If there is a barrier that prevents the attacker from immediately being able to injure or kill you then they are not an imminent threat. If the attacker is behind a secure and solid locked door (no firearm) then he would not be a threat.

Jeopardy: An attacker is acting in such a manner that a reasonable and prudent person would conclude he/she intends to injure or kill.

If the offender/subject has the ability and opportunity to injure or kill you and is acting in a manner that leads you to believe that the person will act out then you are in jeopardy. The attacker/offender/subject is acting in a way that leads you to the conclusion that you are in danger.

Jeopardy can be very subjective in that you have to determine if you are in a "potentially" dangerous situation or "actually" in a dangerous situation. You do not have the ability to know a person's intent as you are not a mind reader. You can only judge the attacker by his appearance, demeanor, actions, and statements that would be consistent with intent to harm you.

Each day we are surrounded by people who have the *ability* to cause us harm, they have the *opportunity* to cause us harm but they do not have the *intent* to hurt us which means that we would not be in jeopardy. The question becomes: Are you in immediate danger? As an officer you need the ability to clearly and accurately articulate why you were in imminent danger which resulted in you being in jeopardy of your life. Specifically, you want to document and articulate what was the attacker saying, doing, and acting that led you to the conclusion that you are in jeopardy.

Preclusion: Officer assessment to determine if a lower level of force would be appropriate or ineffective; and retreat is not possible.

Preclusion means that you have done everything within your power to avoid having to use deadly force without placing yourself or other innocents in jeopardy. Officers are expected to use force as a last resort, when no other options are available, and when tactical retreat is not possible.

Questions to consider:

- What options are available to avoid the need to use force?

- Can you safely retreat without placing yourself in further danger?

Force Options

Once you determine the Elements of Force you are then in a position to determine what level of force, if any, is authorized based on the totality of the circumstances.

Based on the scenario and the elements of force, what level of force on the use of force continuum is reasonable and necessary?

_ Presence

_ Verbal

_ Empty Hand / Personal Weapons

_ OC Spray

_ Impact Weapon / Weapon of Opportunity

_ Lethal Force

It is very important to keep in mind that in a real use of force encounter you must perform all of these functions timely, accurately, effectively and under psychological and physiological reactions of stress. Training is the key!

<u>Training Scenarios</u>

<u>Scenario #1: In-Office Contact</u>

You are in your office sitting at your desk and the parolee is sitting across from you. The parolee is threatening to give you a beating for being disrespectful and is now approaching you at a rapid pace. You have no safety equipment on your person and no way out of the office since you have to get past the parolee to get to the door. Your office is set up so that your back is against the wall and the parolee is closest to the door which is your only exit out of the office.

What do you do?

<u>Elements of Force:</u>

<u>Ability</u> - an attacker possesses the power to injure or kill. This power may come in the form of a weapon (gun, knife, club, etc.) or through disparity of force.

♦ Does the subject have <u>ability</u> to do harm to you as the officer or to a third party?

____ Yes ____ No

<u>Opportunity</u> - an attacker is capable of immediately employing the power to injure or kill. Two components to opportunity are distance and obstacles.

♦ Does the subject have <u>opportunity</u> to do harm to you as the officer or to a third party?

____ Yes ____ No

<u>Jeopardy</u> - an attacker is acting in such a manner that a reasonable and prudent person would conclude he/she intends to injure or kill.

♦ Are you or a third party in jeopardy? ____ Yes ____ No

<u>Preclusion</u> - officer assessment to determine if a lower level of force would be appropriate or ineffective; and retreat is not possible.

What level of force is appropriate?

♦ Is retreat possible? ____ Yes ____ No

Based on the scenario and the elements of force, what level of force on the use of force continuum is reasonable and necessary?

      _ Presence

      _ Verbal

      _ Empty Hand / Personal Weapons

      _ OC Spray

      _ Impact Weapon / Weapon of Opportunity

      _ Lethal Force

Notes: _____

_____

_____

_____

_____

_____

_____

_____

_____

_____

_____

_____

_____

_____

_____

_____

_____

_____

Scenario #2: In-Office Arrest

You are conducting a probation violation arrest in your office. You have handcuffs on your person but no other safety equipment. Two police officers are present when all of a sudden the probationer starts throwing a flurry of kicks and punches at anyone in the vicinity. You were punched in the face and the probationer is now assaulting the police officers.

What do you do?

Elements of Force:

Ability - an attacker possesses the power to injure or kill. This power may come in the form of a weapon (gun, knife, club, etc.) or through disparity of force.

- Does the subject have <u>ability</u> to do harm to you as the officer or to a third party?

    ____ Yes   ____ No

Opportunity - an attacker is capable of immediately employing the power to injure or kill. Two components to opportunity are distance and obstacles.

- Does the subject have <u>opportunity</u> to do harm to you as the officer or to a third party?

    ____ Yes   ____ No

Jeopardy - an attacker is acting in such a manner that a reasonable and prudent person would conclude he/she intends to injure or kill.

- Are you or a third party in jeopardy? ____ Yes   ____ No

Preclusion - officer assessment to determine if a lower level of force would be appropriate or ineffective; and retreat is not possible.

What level of force is appropriate?

- Is retreat possible?   ____ Yes   ____ No

Based on the scenario and the elements of force, what level of force on the use of force continuum is reasonable and necessary?

_ Presence

_ Verbal

_ Empty Hand / Personal Weapons

_ OC Spray

_ Impact Weapon / Weapon of Opportunity

_ Lethal Force

Notes: _____

_____

_____

_____

_____

_____

_____

_____

_____

_____

_____

_____

_____

_____

_____

_____

_____

_____

Scenario #3: In-Office Arrest

You are conducting a PV arrest in your office of your probationer. Per policy you have handcuffs on your person but no other safety equipment. Two police officers are present and the probationer is handcuffed. The probationer states that he is "*going to kill you and give you what you deserve.*"

What do you do?

Elements of Force:

Ability - an attacker possesses the power to injure or kill. This power may come in the form of a weapon (gun, knife, club, etc.) or through disparity of force.

- ◆ Does the subject have <u>ability</u> to do harm to you as the officer or to a third party?

    ____ Yes   ____ No

Opportunity - an attacker is capable of immediately employing the power to injure or kill. Two components to opportunity are distance and obstacles.

- ◆ Does the subject have <u>opportunity</u> to do harm to you as the officer or to a third party?

    ____ Yes   ____ No

Jeopardy - an attacker is acting in such a manner that a reasonable and prudent person would conclude he/she intends to injure or kill.

- ◆ Are you or a third party in jeopardy? ____ Yes   ____ No

Preclusion - officer assessment to determine if a lower level of force would be appropriate or ineffective; and retreat is not possible.

What level of force is appropriate?

- ◆ Is retreat possible?   ____ Yes   ____ No

Based on the scenario and the elements of force, what level of force on the use of force continuum is reasonable and necessary?

_ Presence

_ Verbal

_ Empty Hand / Personal Weapons

_ OC Spray

_ Impact Weapon / Weapon of Opportunity

_ Lethal Force

Notes: _____

_____

_____

_____

_____

_____

_____

_____

_____

_____

_____

_____

_____

_____

_____

_____

_____

<u>Scenario #4: Field Contact</u>

You are conducting an unscheduled field contact. You are alone inside the residence and the parolee says you are not leaving. You politely ask the parolee to move away from the front door so you can exit but he blocks the door and is staring at you. You have all of your safety equipment but no firearm.

What do you do?

<u>Elements of Force:</u>

Ability - an attacker possesses the power to injure or kill. This power may come in the form of a weapon (gun, knife, club, etc.) or through disparity of force.

♦ Does the subject have <u>ability</u> to do harm to you as the officer or to a third party?

_____ Yes   _____ No

Opportunity - an attacker is capable of immediately employing the power to injure or kill. Two components to opportunity are distance and obstacles.

♦ Does the subject have <u>opportunity</u> to do harm to you as the officer or to a third party?

_____ Yes   _____ No

Jeopardy - an attacker is acting in such a manner that a reasonable and prudent person would conclude he/she intends to injure or kill.

♦ Are you or a third party in jeopardy? _____ Yes   _____ No

Preclusion - officer assessment to determine if a lower level of force would be appropriate or ineffective; and retreat is not possible.

What level of force is appropriate?

♦ Is retreat possible?   _____ Yes   _____ No

Based on the scenario and the elements of force, what level of force on the use of force continuum is reasonable and necessary?

    _ Presence

    _ Verbal

    _ Empty Hand / Personal Weapons

    _ OC Spray

    _ Impact Weapon / Weapon of Opportunity

    _ Lethal Force

Notes: _____

_____

_____

_____

_____

_____

_____

_____

_____

_____

_____

_____

_____

_____

_____

_____

_____

_____

Scenario #5: Field Arrest

You are conducting a field arrest of your probationer and the police are present. The probationer is handcuffed and in custody. As the probationer is about to be placed in the police car he says he wants to ask you a question about the probation violation. When you approach to hear the question he kicks you in the groin which drops you to the ground. He then spits on you. The probationer does not attempt to hit you again.

What do you do?

<u>Elements of Force:</u>

<u>Ability</u> - an attacker possesses the power to injure or kill. This power may come in the form of a weapon (gun, knife, club, etc.) or through disparity of force.

- ◆ Does the subject have <u>ability</u> to do harm to you as the officer or to a third party?

    _____ Yes   _____ No

<u>Opportunity</u> - an attacker is capable of immediately employing the power to injure or kill. Two components to opportunity are distance and obstacles.

- ◆ Does the subject have <u>opportunity</u> to do harm to you as the officer or to a third party?

    _____ Yes   _____ No

<u>Jeopardy</u> - an attacker is acting in such a manner that a reasonable and prudent person would conclude he/she intends to injure or kill.

- ◆ Are you or a third party in jeopardy? _____ Yes   _____ No

<u>Preclusion</u> - officer assessment to determine if a lower level of force would be appropriate or ineffective; and retreat is not possible.

    What level of force is appropriate?

- ◆ Is retreat possible?   _____ Yes   _____ No

Based on the scenario and the elements of force, what level of force on the use of force continuum is reasonable and necessary?

    _ Presence

    _ Verbal

    _ Empty Hand / Personal Weapons

    _ OC Spray

    _ Impact Weapon / Weapon of Opportunity

    _ Lethal Force

Notes: _____

_____

_____

_____

_____

_____

_____

_____

_____

_____

_____

_____

_____

_____

_____

_____

_____

_____

_____

Scenario #6: Partner Attacked

You are working as a backup partner with your office mate conducting a field contact. As the backup officer you are scanning the environment for potential safety concerns when all of a sudden your partner is being violently attacked by the parolee. The parolee is not using any weapons other than kicks and punches.

What do you do?

Elements of Force:

Ability - an attacker possesses the power to injure or kill. This power may come in the form of a weapon (gun, knife, club, etc.) or through disparity of force.

♦ Does the subject have <u>ability</u> to do harm to you as the officer or to a third party?

_____ Yes   _____ No

Opportunity - an attacker is capable of immediately employing the power to injure or kill. Two components to opportunity are distance and obstacles.

♦ Does the subject have <u>opportunity</u> to do harm to you as the officer or to a third party?

_____ Yes   _____ No

Jeopardy - an attacker is acting in such a manner that a reasonable and prudent person would conclude he/she intends to injure or kill.

♦ Are you or a third party in jeopardy? _____ Yes   _____ No

Preclusion - officer assessment to determine if a lower level of force would be appropriate or ineffective; and retreat is not possible.

What level of force is appropriate?

♦ Is retreat possible?   _____ Yes   _____ No

Based on the scenario and the elements of force, what level of force on the use of force continuum is reasonable and necessary?

_ Presence

_ Verbal

_ Empty Hand / Personal Weapons

_ OC Spray

_ Impact Weapon / Weapon of Opportunity

_ Lethal Force

Notes: _____

_____

_____

_____

_____

_____

_____

_____

_____

_____

_____

_____

_____

_____

_____

_____

_____

_____

_____

<u>Scenario #7: Family Dynamics</u>

You are alone conducting a field contact. You are talking with a female probationer when her husband and son enter the home. The father starts yelling at his son and slaps him in the face multiple times. You have no idea why the father is hitting his son. The father does not pay any attention to the fact you are at the residence.

What do you do?

<u>Elements of Force:</u>

Ability - an attacker possesses the power to injure or kill. This power may come in the form of a weapon (gun, knife, club, etc.) or through disparity of force.

- ◆ Does the subject have <u>ability</u> to do harm to you as the officer or to a third party?

    _____ Yes   _____ No

Opportunity - an attacker is capable of immediately employing the power to injure or kill. Two components to opportunity are distance and obstacles.

- ◆ Does the subject have <u>opportunity</u> to do harm to you as the officer or to a third party?

    _____ Yes   _____ No

Jeopardy - an attacker is acting in such a manner that a reasonable and prudent person would conclude he/she intends to injure or kill.

- ◆ Are you or a third party in jeopardy? _____ Yes   _____ No

Preclusion - officer assessment to determine if a lower level of force would be appropriate or ineffective; and retreat is not possible.

    What level of force is appropriate?

- ◆ Is retreat possible?   _____ Yes   _____ No

Based on the scenario and the elements of force, what level of force on the use of force continuum is reasonable and necessary?

_ Presence

_ Verbal

_ Empty Hand / Personal Weapons

_ OC Spray

_ Impact Weapon / Weapon of Opportunity

_ Lethal Force

Notes: _____

_____

_____

_____

_____

_____

_____

_____

_____

_____

_____

_____

_____

_____

_____

_____

_____

_____

_____

Scenario #8: Convenience Store Robbery

You are alone conducting field work when you decide to buy a drink at Circle K. As you are getting your drink two men enter the store with guns and rob the clerk. One of the gunmen is controlling the front door so exiting the store is not possible. You are an armed officer with all of your safety equipment on your person. You are also wearing body armor and your weapon is concealed.

What do you do?

<u>Elements of Force:</u>

Ability - an attacker possesses the power to injure or kill. This power may come in the form of a weapon (gun, knife, club, etc.) or through disparity of force.

  ♦   Does the subject have <u>ability</u> to do harm to you as the officer or to a third party?

    ____ Yes   ____ No

Opportunity - an attacker is capable of immediately employing the power to injure or kill. Two components to opportunity are distance and obstacles.

  ♦   Does the subject have <u>opportunity</u> to do harm to you as the officer or to a third party?

    ____ Yes   ____ No

Jeopardy - an attacker is acting in such a manner that a reasonable and prudent person would conclude he/she intends to injure or kill.

  ♦   Are you or a third party in jeopardy? ____ Yes   ____ No

Preclusion - officer assessment to determine if a lower level of force would be appropriate or ineffective; and retreat is not possible.

    What level of force is appropriate?

  ♦   Is retreat possible?   ____ Yes   ____ No

Based on the scenario and the elements of force, what level of force on the use of force continuum is reasonable and necessary?

_ Presence

_ Verbal

_ Empty Hand / Personal Weapons

_ OC Spray

_ Impact Weapon / Weapon of Opportunity

_ Lethal Force

Notes: _____

_____

_____

_____

_____

_____

_____

_____

_____

_____

_____

_____

_____

_____

_____

_____

_____

_____

_____

Scenario #9: Gunpoint in the Office

You are an armed officer walking down a hallway by your office early in the morning. There are very few other staff members in the building due to the early time. You see a probationer pointing a gun at his PO's head. The probationer with the gun sees you and tells you to "*get over here now*" as he points the gun at you. You do not have time to obtain cover or concealment. You are now with the other officer and both of you are at gunpoint.

What do you do?

Elements of Force:

Ability - an attacker possesses the power to injure or kill. This power may come in the form of a weapon (gun, knife, club, etc.) or through disparity of force.

♦ Does the subject have <u>ability</u> to do harm to you as the officer or to a third party?

_____ Yes   _____ No

Opportunity - an attacker is capable of immediately employing the power to injure or kill. Two components to opportunity are distance and obstacles.

♦ Does the subject have <u>opportunity</u> to do harm to you as the officer or to a third party?

_____ Yes   _____ No

Jeopardy - an attacker is acting in such a manner that a reasonable and prudent person would conclude he/she intends to injure or kill.

♦ Are you or a third party in jeopardy? _____ Yes   _____ No

Preclusion - officer assessment to determine if a lower level of force would be appropriate or ineffective; and retreat is not possible.

What level of force is appropriate?

♦ Is retreat possible?   _____ Yes   _____ No

Based on the scenario and the elements of force, what level of force on the use of force continuum is reasonable and necessary?

　　　_ Presence

　　　_ Verbal

　　　_ Empty Hand / Personal Weapons

　　　_ OC Spray

　　　_ Impact Weapon / Weapon of Opportunity

　　　_ Lethal Force

Notes: _____

_____

_____

_____

_____

_____

_____

_____

_____

_____

_____

_____

_____

_____

_____

_____

_____

_____

_____

Officer Survival Training Scenarios

Scenario #10: Residential Search

You are conducting a residential search based on information that the probationer has weapons at the house. You have a search team present along with enough police officers. The police handcuff the probationer behind the back and sit him on the couch. While handcuffed the probationer grabs a hidden .45 caliber gun from the couch and shoots a police officer in the head and then continues to fire at everyone in the room which includes you. You are an armed officer.

What do you do?

Elements of Force:

Ability - an attacker possesses the power to injure or kill. This power may come in the form of a weapon (gun, knife, club, etc.) or through disparity of force.

- ◆ Does the subject have <u>ability</u> to do harm to you as the officer or to a third party?

  _____ Yes   _____ No

Opportunity - an attacker is capable of immediately employing the power to injure or kill. Two components to opportunity are distance and obstacles.

- ◆ Does the subject have <u>opportunity</u> to do harm to you as the officer or to a third party?

  _____ Yes   _____ No

Jeopardy - an attacker is acting in such a manner that a reasonable and prudent person would conclude he/she intends to injure or kill.

- ◆ Are you or a third party in jeopardy? _____ Yes   _____ No

Preclusion - officer assessment to determine if a lower level of force would be appropriate or ineffective; and retreat is not possible.

  What level of force is appropriate?

- ◆ Is retreat possible?   _____ Yes   _____ No

Based on the scenario and the elements of force, what level of force on the use of force continuum is reasonable and necessary?

    _ Presence

    _ Verbal

    _ Empty Hand / Personal Weapons

    _ OC Spray

    _ Impact Weapon / Weapon of Opportunity

    _ Lethal Force

Notes: _____

_____

_____

_____

_____

_____

_____

_____

_____

_____

_____

_____

_____

_____

_____

_____

_____

_____

Scenario #11: Driving to Work

You are driving to the office when a car pulls in front of you forcing you to stop. A man jumps out of the car and is rapidly approaching your car door. There is a car behind you so you can't back up. Your door is locked so this person breaks your window as he is screaming and punching at you. You are an armed officer but do not have any other safety equipment on your person. *(You don't realize it at the time but this is an ex-probationer that you sent to prison for 3 years for a probation violation and he was released last week.)*

What do you do?

Elements of Force:

Ability - an attacker possesses the power to injure or kill. This power may come in the form of a weapon (gun, knife, club, etc.) or through disparity of force.

  ♦   Does the subject have <u>ability</u> to do harm to you as the officer or to a third party?

  _____ Yes   _____ No

Opportunity - an attacker is capable of immediately employing the power to injure or kill. Two components to opportunity are distance and obstacles.

  ♦   Does the subject have <u>opportunity</u> to do harm to you as the officer or to a third party?

  _____ Yes   _____ No

Jeopardy - an attacker is acting in such a manner that a reasonable and prudent person would conclude he/she intends to injure or kill.

  ♦   Are you or a third party in jeopardy? _____ Yes   _____ No

Preclusion - officer assessment to determine if a lower level of force would be appropriate or ineffective; and retreat is not possible.

  What level of force is appropriate?

  ♦   Is retreat possible?   _____ Yes   _____ No

Based on the scenario and the elements of force, what level of force on the use of force continuum is reasonable and necessary?

_ Presence

_ Verbal

_ Empty Hand / Personal Weapons

_ OC Spray

_ Impact Weapon / Weapon of Opportunity

_ Lethal Force

Notes: _____

_____

_____

_____

_____

_____

_____

_____

_____

_____

_____

_____

_____

_____

_____

_____

_____

_____

<u>Scenario #12: Juvenile Residential Contact</u>

You are conducting a home contact on a 16 year old male assigned to your caseload. The juveniles mother is home. You enter the residence and the juvenile starts walking toward his bedroom and asks you to follow. As you enter the bedroom the juvenile is sitting on his bed when you notice the grip of a handgun under his pillow.

What do you do?

<u>**Elements of Force:**</u>

<u>**Ability**</u> - an attacker possesses the power to injure or kill. This power may come in the form of a weapon (gun, knife, club, etc.) or through disparity of force.

- ◆ Does the subject have <u>ability</u> to do harm to you as the officer or to a third party?

     ____ Yes   ____ No

<u>**Opportunity**</u> - an attacker is capable of immediately employing the power to injure or kill. Two components to opportunity are distance and obstacles.

- ◆ Does the subject have <u>opportunity</u> to do harm to you as the officer or to a third party?

     ____ Yes   ____ No

<u>**Jeopardy**</u> - an attacker is acting in such a manner that a reasonable and prudent person would conclude he/she intends to injure or kill.

- ◆ Are you or a third party in jeopardy? ____ Yes   ____ No

<u>**Preclusion**</u> - officer assessment to determine if a lower level of force would be appropriate or ineffective; and retreat is not possible.

     What level of force is appropriate?

- ◆ Is retreat possible?   ____ Yes   ____ No

Based on the scenario and the elements of force, what level of force on the use of force continuum is reasonable and necessary?

  _ Presence

  _ Verbal

  _ Empty Hand / Personal Weapons

  _ OC Spray

  _ Impact Weapon / Weapon of Opportunity

  _ Lethal Force

Notes: _____

_____

_____

_____

_____

_____

_____

_____

_____

_____

_____

_____

_____

_____

_____

_____

_____

_____

_____

Scenario #13: Juvenile Residential Contact

You are conducting a home contact on a 15 year old bipolar female assigned to your caseload. The juvenile is home alone and asks you to come in stating that she really needs your help. She sits on the living room sofa and tells you that she just swallowed a full bottle of Lithium medication.

What do you do?

Elements of Force:

Ability - an attacker possesses the power to injure or kill. This power may come in the form of a weapon (gun, knife, club, etc.) or through disparity of force.

  ♦ Does the subject have <u>ability</u> to do harm to you as the officer or to a third party?

   _____ Yes   _____ No

Opportunity - an attacker is capable of immediately employing the power to injure or kill. Two components to opportunity are distance and obstacles.

  ♦ Does the subject have <u>opportunity</u> to do harm to you as the officer or to a third party?

   _____ Yes   _____ No

Jeopardy - an attacker is acting in such a manner that a reasonable and prudent person would conclude he/she intends to injure or kill.

  ♦ Are you or a third party in jeopardy? _____ Yes   _____ No

Preclusion - officer assessment to determine if a lower level of force would be appropriate or ineffective; and retreat is not possible.

   What level of force is appropriate?

  ♦ Is retreat possible?   _____ Yes   _____ No

Based on the scenario and the elements of force, what level of force on the use of force continuum is reasonable and necessary?

    _ Presence

    _ Verbal

    _ Empty Hand / Personal Weapons

    _ OC Spray

    _ Impact Weapon / Weapon of Opportunity

    _ Lethal Force

Notes: _____

_____

_____

_____

_____

_____

_____

_____

_____

_____

_____

_____

_____

_____

_____

_____

_____

_____

Scenario #14: Sadistic Sex Offender

You are conducting a home contact on a 45 year old sex offender who is on lifetime probation. He served a prison sentence for sexual assault on 4 teenage boys. It is 9:03PM when you ring the doorbell but the offender does not answer. You notice light is shining through the front window when you decide to look inside. On the living room sofa is a teenage boy who is naked, bound and gagged. You see the offender, who is naked, brutally beating the boy. You pound on the door but he does not answer. Instead, the offender grabs the boy and moves him to a room that is out of view. The teenage boy is clearly in jeopardy.

What do you do?

Elements of Force:

Ability - an attacker possesses the power to injure or kill. This power may come in the form of a weapon (gun, knife, club, etc.) or through disparity of force.

♦ Does the subject have <u>ability</u> to do harm to you as the officer or to a third party?

_____ Yes   _____ No

Opportunity - an attacker is capable of immediately employing the power to injure or kill. Two components to opportunity are distance and obstacles.

♦ Does the subject have <u>opportunity</u> to do harm to you as the officer or to a third party?

_____ Yes   _____ No

Jeopardy - an attacker is acting in such a manner that a reasonable and prudent person would conclude he/she intends to injure or kill.

♦ Are you or a third party in jeopardy? _____ Yes   _____ No

Preclusion - officer assessment to determine if a lower level of force would be appropriate or ineffective; and retreat is not possible.

What level of force is appropriate?

♦ Is retreat possible? _____ Yes   _____ No

45

Scott Kirshner

Based on the scenario and the elements of force, what level of force on the use of force continuum is reasonable and necessary?

_ Presence

_ Verbal

_ Empty Hand / Personal Weapons

_ OC Spray

_ Impact Weapon / Weapon of Opportunity

_ Lethal Force

Notes: _____

_____

_____

_____

_____

_____

_____

_____

_____

_____

_____

_____

_____

_____

_____

_____

_____

Scenario #15: Home Contact – At Your Home!

You are leaving your house at 7:00AM to go to work. As you get to the end of your street you notice a parked car with an offender who is assigned to your caseload. He makes a gesture with his hand as if he is going to shoot you. You drive away to see what he is going to do but he does not follow you. At home are your spouse and children.

What do you do?

Elements of Force:

Ability - an attacker possesses the power to injure or kill. This power may come in the form of a weapon (gun, knife, club, etc.) or through disparity of force.

- ♦ Does the subject have <u>ability</u> to do harm to you as the officer or to a third party?

    _____ Yes   _____ No

Opportunity - an attacker is capable of immediately employing the power to injure or kill. Two components to opportunity are distance and obstacles.

- ♦ Does the subject have <u>opportunity</u> to do harm to you as the officer or to a third party?

    _____ Yes   _____ No

Jeopardy - an attacker is acting in such a manner that a reasonable and prudent person would conclude he/she intends to injure or kill.

- ♦ Are you or a third party in jeopardy? _____ Yes   _____ No

Preclusion - officer assessment to determine if a lower level of force would be appropriate or ineffective; and retreat is not possible.

    What level of force is appropriate?

- ♦ Is retreat possible?   _____ Yes   _____ No

Based on the scenario and the elements of force, what level of force on the use of force continuum is reasonable and necessary?

    _ Presence

    _ Verbal

    _ Empty Hand / Personal Weapons

    _ OC Spray

    _ Impact Weapon / Weapon of Opportunity

    _ Lethal Force

Notes: _____

_____

_____

_____

_____

_____

_____

_____

_____

_____

_____

_____

_____

_____

_____

_____

_____

Scenario #16: Domestic Violence Group Counseling

You are conducting a check at a domestic violence group class where you have a few high risk domestic violence offenders assigned. When you arrive the group is on break and a bunch of offenders are outside smoking. You want to ask the group facilitator how the offenders are doing but when you approach a couple of offenders start verbally harassing you. They are calling you a pig and making a snorting noise.

What do you do?

Elements of Force:

Ability - an attacker possesses the power to injure or kill. This power may come in the form of a weapon (gun, knife, club, etc.) or through disparity of force.

- ♦ Does the subject have <u>ability</u> to do harm to you as the officer or to a third party?

  _____ Yes   _____ No

Opportunity - an attacker is capable of immediately employing the power to injure or kill. Two components to opportunity are distance and obstacles.

- ♦ Does the subject have <u>opportunity</u> to do harm to you as the officer or to a third party?

  _____ Yes   _____ No

Jeopardy - an attacker is acting in such a manner that a reasonable and prudent person would conclude he/she intends to injure or kill.

- ♦ Are you or a third party in jeopardy? _____ Yes   _____ No

Preclusion - officer assessment to determine if a lower level of force would be appropriate or ineffective; and retreat is not possible.

  What level of force is appropriate?

- ♦ Is retreat possible?   _____ Yes   _____ No

Based on the scenario and the elements of force, what level of force on the use of force continuum is reasonable and necessary?

_ Presence

_ Verbal

_ Empty Hand / Personal Weapons

_ OC Spray

_ Impact Weapon / Weapon of Opportunity

_ Lethal Force

Notes: _____

_____

_____

_____

_____

_____

_____

_____

_____

_____

_____

_____

_____

_____

_____

_____

_____

_____

_____

Scenario #17: Offender Assessment

You are with an offender in an interview room conducting an offender assessment screening tool. This assessment will help you develop a case management plan and behavior contract with the offender. The interview room is equipped with a duress/panic button. As you are asking the offender questions he is becoming visibly upset. All of a sudden he jumps up and throws the chair he was sitting on which hits you in the face.

What do you do?

Elements of Force:

Ability - an attacker possesses the power to injure or kill. This power may come in the form of a weapon (gun, knife, club, etc.) or through disparity of force.

- ♦ Does the subject have <u>ability</u> to do harm to you as the officer or to a third party?

    _____ Yes   _____ No

Opportunity - an attacker is capable of immediately employing the power to injure or kill. Two components to opportunity are distance and obstacles.

- ♦ Does the subject have <u>opportunity</u> to do harm to you as the officer or to a third party?

    _____ Yes   _____ No

Jeopardy - an attacker is acting in such a manner that a reasonable and prudent person would conclude he/she intends to injure or kill.

- ♦ Are you or a third party in jeopardy? _____ Yes   _____ No

Preclusion - officer assessment to determine if a lower level of force would be appropriate or ineffective; and retreat is not possible.

    What level of force is appropriate?

- ♦ Is retreat possible?   _____ Yes   _____ No

Based on the scenario and the elements of force, what level of force on the use of force continuum is reasonable and necessary?

_ Presence

_ Verbal

_ Empty Hand / Personal Weapons

_ OC Spray

_ Impact Weapon / Weapon of Opportunity

_ Lethal Force

Notes: _____

_____

_____

_____

_____

_____

_____

_____

_____

_____

_____

_____

_____

_____

_____

_____

_____

Scenario #18: Positive Drug Test

An offender is sitting in your office due to three positive drug tests for methamphetamine and marijuana. You tell the offender you are willing to work with him but that he needs to attend intensive outpatient treatment. The offender is sitting quietly in his chair staring at the ground. He is not saying a word and is not responsive to your input. You notice that his face is turning beat red, he is clenching his teeth and making a fist with both hands.

What do you do?

<u>Elements of Force:</u>

Ability - an attacker possesses the power to injure or kill. This power may come in the form of a weapon (gun, knife, club, etc.) or through disparity of force.

- ♦ Does the subject have <u>ability</u> to do harm to you as the officer or to a third party?

    _____ Yes   _____ No

Opportunity - an attacker is capable of immediately employing the power to injure or kill. Two components to opportunity are distance and obstacles.

- ♦ Does the subject have <u>opportunity</u> to do harm to you as the officer or to a third party?

    _____ Yes   _____ No

Jeopardy - an attacker is acting in such a manner that a reasonable and prudent person would conclude he/she intends to injure or kill.

- ♦ Are you or a third party in jeopardy? _____ Yes   _____ No

Preclusion - officer assessment to determine if a lower level of force would be appropriate or ineffective; and retreat is not possible.

    What level of force is appropriate?

- ♦ Is retreat possible?   _____ Yes   _____ No

Based on the scenario and the elements of force, what level of force on the use of force continuum is reasonable and necessary?

_ Presence

_ Verbal

_ Empty Hand / Personal Weapons

_ OC Spray

_ Impact Weapon / Weapon of Opportunity

_ Lethal Force

Notes: _____

_____

_____

_____

_____

_____

_____

_____

_____

_____

_____

_____

_____

_____

_____

_____

_____

_____

Scenario #19: Waiting Room Fight

You walk to the parole office waiting room door to call your offender back to the interview room for his monthly contact. As you open the door you see your offender punch another offender in the face knocking him out. The knocked out offender falls to the ground unconscious as your offender is repeatedly kicking him in the head.

What do you do?

Elements of Force:

Ability - an attacker possesses the power to injure or kill. This power may come in the form of a weapon (gun, knife, club, etc.) or through disparity of force.

- Does the subject have ability to do harm to you as the officer or to a third party?

    ____ Yes   ____ No

Opportunity - an attacker is capable of immediately employing the power to injure or kill. Two components to opportunity are distance and obstacles.

- Does the subject have opportunity to do harm to you as the officer or to a third party?

    ____ Yes   ____ No

Jeopardy - an attacker is acting in such a manner that a reasonable and prudent person would conclude he/she intends to injure or kill.

- Are you or a third party in jeopardy? ____ Yes   ____ No

Preclusion - officer assessment to determine if a lower level of force would be appropriate or ineffective; and retreat is not possible.

    What level of force is appropriate?

- Is retreat possible?   ____ Yes   ____ No

Based on the scenario and the elements of force, what level of force on the use of force continuum is reasonable and necessary?

    _ Presence

    _ Verbal

    _ Empty Hand / Personal Weapons

    _ OC Spray

    _ Impact Weapon / Weapon of Opportunity

    _ Lethal Force

Notes: _____

_____

_____

_____

_____

_____

_____

_____

_____

_____

_____

_____

_____

_____

_____

_____

_____

_____

<u>Scenario #20: Escort Gone Bad</u>

You are escorting an offender back to the interview room. The offender has been non-compliant recently and you are going to discuss a course of action. The offender is about three feet in front of you when he explosively turns around and attacks you without warning. The attack is brutal, violent and non-stop.

What do you do?

<u>Elements of Force:</u>

Ability - an attacker possesses the power to injure or kill. This power may come in the form of a weapon (gun, knife, club, etc.) or through disparity of force.

- Does the subject have <u>ability</u> to do harm to you as the officer or to a third party?

    _____ Yes   _____ No

Opportunity - an attacker is capable of immediately employing the power to injure or kill. Two components to opportunity are distance and obstacles.

- Does the subject have <u>opportunity</u> to do harm to you as the officer or to a third party?

    _____ Yes   _____ No

Jeopardy - an attacker is acting in such a manner that a reasonable and prudent person would conclude he/she intends to injure or kill.

- Are you or a third party in jeopardy? _____ Yes   _____ No

Preclusion - officer assessment to determine if a lower level of force would be appropriate or ineffective; and retreat is not possible.

    What level of force is appropriate?

- Is retreat possible?   _____ Yes   _____ No

Based on the scenario and the elements of force, what level of force on the use of force continuum is reasonable and necessary?

_ Presence

_ Verbal

_ Empty Hand / Personal Weapons

_ OC Spray

_ Impact Weapon / Weapon of Opportunity

_ Lethal Force

Notes: _____

_____

_____

_____

_____

_____

_____

_____

_____

_____

_____

_____

_____

_____

_____

_____

_____

_____

_____

Scenario #21: Active Shooter

It is late in the day and you are documenting notes into your offender database. Your parole office has security guards and a weapons screening process. Out of nowhere you hear multiple gunshots that are very loud followed by screaming and chaos. You have no idea what is going on or who fired the shots.

What do you do?

Elements of Force:

Ability - an attacker possesses the power to injure or kill. This power may come in the form of a weapon (gun, knife, club, etc.) or through disparity of force.

- Does the subject have <u>ability</u> to do harm to you as the officer or to a third party?

    ____ Yes   ____ No

Opportunity - an attacker is capable of immediately employing the power to injure or kill. Two components to opportunity are distance and obstacles.

- Does the subject have <u>opportunity</u> to do harm to you as the officer or to a third party?

    ____ Yes   ____ No

Jeopardy - an attacker is acting in such a manner that a reasonable and prudent person would conclude he/she intends to injure or kill.

- Are you or a third party in jeopardy? ____ Yes   ____ No

Preclusion - officer assessment to determine if a lower level of force would be appropriate or ineffective; and retreat is not possible.

    What level of force is appropriate?

- Is retreat possible?   ____ Yes   ____ No

Based on the scenario and the elements of force, what level of force on the use of force continuum is reasonable and necessary?

      _ Presence

      _ Verbal

      _ Empty Hand / Personal Weapons

      _ OC Spray

      _ Impact Weapon / Weapon of Opportunity

      _ Lethal Force

Notes: _____

_____

_____

_____

_____

_____

_____

_____

_____

_____

_____

_____

_____

_____

_____

_____

_____

_____

Scenario #22: Gunshots in the Office

You are staffing a case with your parole supervisor regarding an offender that is having behavioral problems. Out of nowhere you hear someone yell, *"gun, he has a gun"* followed by three rapid fire shots. You do not know if an officer fired the shots or an offender.

What do you do?

Elements of Force:

Ability - an attacker possesses the power to injure or kill. This power may come in the form of a weapon (gun, knife, club, etc.) or through disparity of force.

- Does the subject have <u>ability</u> to do harm to you as the officer or to a third party?

    _____ Yes   _____ No

Opportunity - an attacker is capable of immediately employing the power to injure or kill. Two components to opportunity are distance and obstacles.

- Does the subject have <u>opportunity</u> to do harm to you as the officer or to a third party?

    _____ Yes   _____ No

Jeopardy - an attacker is acting in such a manner that a reasonable and prudent person would conclude he/she intends to injure or kill.

- Are you or a third party in jeopardy? _____ Yes   _____ No

Preclusion - officer assessment to determine if a lower level of force would be appropriate or ineffective; and retreat is not possible.

What level of force is appropriate?

- Is retreat possible?   _____ Yes   _____ No

Based on the scenario and the elements of force, what level of force on the use of force continuum is reasonable and necessary?

_ Presence

_ Verbal

_ Empty Hand / Personal Weapons

_ OC Spray

_ Impact Weapon / Weapon of Opportunity

_ Lethal Force

Notes: _____

_____

_____

_____

_____

_____

_____

_____

_____

_____

_____

_____

_____

_____

_____

_____

_____

_____

Scenario #23: "I got your license plate number"

You are conducting a field contact at an apartment complex known for drug activity and violence. You have a partner with you and the contact goes well. You are driving your personal vehicle. As you both walk back to your vehicle there is a man in his 30's leaning on your car. As you approach he calmly says, *"I got your license plate number and that will tell me all I need."*

What do you do?

Elements of Force:

Ability - an attacker possesses the power to injure or kill. This power may come in the form of a weapon (gun, knife, club, etc.) or through disparity of force.

♦ Does the subject have <u>ability</u> to do harm to you as the officer or to a third party?

_____ Yes   _____ No

Opportunity - an attacker is capable of immediately employing the power to injure or kill. Two components to opportunity are distance and obstacles.

♦ Does the subject have <u>opportunity</u> to do harm to you as the officer or to a third party?

_____ Yes   _____ No

Jeopardy - an attacker is acting in such a manner that a reasonable and prudent person would conclude he/she intends to injure or kill.

♦ Are you or a third party in jeopardy? _____ Yes   _____ No

Preclusion - officer assessment to determine if a lower level of force would be appropriate or ineffective; and retreat is not possible.

What level of force is appropriate?

♦ Is retreat possible?   _____ Yes   _____ No

Based on the scenario and the elements of force, what level of force on the use of force continuum is reasonable and necessary?

    _ Presence

    _ Verbal

    _ Empty Hand / Personal Weapons

    _ OC Spray

    _ Impact Weapon / Weapon of Opportunity

    _ Lethal Force

Notes: _____

_____

_____

_____

_____

_____

_____

_____

_____

_____

_____

_____

_____

_____

_____

_____

_____

_____

Scenario #24: Police Officer in Jeopardy

You are conducting field work with a partner. You stop at a local fast food restaurant to eat lunch. As you are sitting at your table and eating you notice a police officer outside the restaurant is being attacked by a subject during a vehicle stop. The police officer is on the ground, appears hurt and needs immediate help.

What do you do?

Elements of Force:

Ability - an attacker possesses the power to injure or kill. This power may come in the form of a weapon (gun, knife, club, etc.) or through disparity of force.

- ♦ Does the subject have <u>ability</u> to do harm to you as the officer or to a third party?

    _____ Yes   _____ No

Opportunity - an attacker is capable of immediately employing the power to injure or kill. Two components to opportunity are distance and obstacles.

- ♦ Does the subject have <u>opportunity</u> to do harm to you as the officer or to a third party?

    _____ Yes   _____ No

Jeopardy - an attacker is acting in such a manner that a reasonable and prudent person would conclude he/she intends to injure or kill.

- ♦ Are you or a third party in jeopardy? _____ Yes   _____ No

Preclusion - officer assessment to determine if a lower level of force would be appropriate or ineffective; and retreat is not possible.

    What level of force is appropriate?

- ♦ Is retreat possible?   _____ Yes   _____ No

Scott Kirshner

Based on the scenario and the elements of force, what level of force on the use of force continuum is reasonable and necessary?

    _ Presence

    _ Verbal

    _ Empty Hand / Personal Weapons

    _ OC Spray

    _ Impact Weapon / Weapon of Opportunity

    _ Lethal Force

Notes: _____

_____

_____

_____

_____

_____

_____

_____

_____

_____

_____

_____

_____

_____

_____

_____

_____

Scenario #25: Knife

You are conducting a field contact at a parolees apartment. After you knock the parolee answers the front door. You ask if anyone else is home and she responds, "no." She says come inside which you do. After you enter the apartment the offender sits on the couch. You sit on a chair across from her. She appears calm, friendly and engaged. She then calmly stands up, goes to the front door and locks it. You ask what she is doing when she pulls out a 6 inch knife and starts to aggressively walk toward you not saying a word.

What do you do?

Elements of Force:

Ability - an attacker possesses the power to injure or kill. This power may come in the form of a weapon (gun, knife, club, etc.) or through disparity of force.

♦ Does the subject have <u>ability</u> to do harm to you as the officer or to a third party?

____ Yes ____ No

Opportunity - an attacker is capable of immediately employing the power to injure or kill. Two components to opportunity are distance and obstacles.

♦ Does the subject have <u>opportunity</u> to do harm to you as the officer or to a third party?

____ Yes ____ No

Jeopardy - an attacker is acting in such a manner that a reasonable and prudent person would conclude he/she intends to injure or kill.

♦ Are you or a third party in jeopardy? ____ Yes ____ No

Preclusion - officer assessment to determine if a lower level of force would be appropriate or ineffective; and retreat is not possible.

What level of force is appropriate?

♦ Is retreat possible? ____ Yes ____ No

Based on the scenario and the elements of force, what level of force on the use of force continuum is reasonable and necessary?

_ Presence

_ Verbal

_ Empty Hand / Personal Weapons

_ OC Spray

_ Impact Weapon / Weapon of Opportunity

_ Lethal Force

Notes: _____

_____

_____

_____

_____

_____

_____

_____

_____

_____

_____

_____

_____

_____

_____

_____

_____

_____

Scenario #26: Problems

You are conducting an office contact on an offender who recently lost his job and his wife left him. He is stressed and appears to be falling apart emotionally. He is not aggressive toward you but hints that hurting an officer to go back to prison might not be such a bad option.

What do you do?

Elements of Force:

Ability - an attacker possesses the power to injure or kill. This power may come in the form of a weapon (gun, knife, club, etc.) or through disparity of force.

   ♦   Does the subject have <u>ability</u> to do harm to you as the officer or to a third party?

   _____ Yes   _____ No

Opportunity - an attacker is capable of immediately employing the power to injure or kill. Two components to opportunity are distance and obstacles.

   ♦   Does the subject have <u>opportunity</u> to do harm to you as the officer or to a third party?

   _____ Yes   _____ No

Jeopardy - an attacker is acting in such a manner that a reasonable and prudent person would conclude he/she intends to injure or kill.

   ♦   Are you or a third party in jeopardy? _____ Yes   _____ No

Preclusion - officer assessment to determine if a lower level of force would be appropriate or ineffective; and retreat is not possible.

   What level of force is appropriate?

   ♦   Is retreat possible?   _____ Yes   _____ No

Scott Kirshner

Based on the scenario and the elements of force, what level of force on the use of force continuum is reasonable and necessary?

     _ Presence

     _ Verbal

     _ Empty Hand / Personal Weapons

     _ OC Spray

     _ Impact Weapon / Weapon of Opportunity

     _ Lethal Force

Notes: _____

_____

_____

_____

_____

_____

_____

_____

_____

_____

_____

_____

_____

_____

_____

_____

_____

Scenario #27: Veiled Threats

You write up an offender with a violation warning for non-compliant behavior. You tell the offender that this is his last chance before getting arrested. The offender tells you to, "*Reconsider your words officer as I know where you and your family live. And, even if I am locked up I can reach out and touch you.*" The offender then smiles but it is just a cover. He got his message across loud and clear.

What do you do?

Elements of Force:

Ability - an attacker possesses the power to injure or kill. This power may come in the form of a weapon (gun, knife, club, etc.) or through disparity of force.

  ♦ Does the subject have <u>ability</u> to do harm to you as the officer or to a third party?

  _____ Yes   _____ No

Opportunity - an attacker is capable of immediately employing the power to injure or kill. Two components to opportunity are distance and obstacles.

  ♦ Does the subject have <u>opportunity</u> to do harm to you as the officer or to a third party?

  _____ Yes   _____ No

Jeopardy - an attacker is acting in such a manner that a reasonable and prudent person would conclude he/she intends to injure or kill.

  ♦ Are you or a third party in jeopardy? _____ Yes   _____ No

Preclusion - officer assessment to determine if a lower level of force would be appropriate or ineffective; and retreat is not possible.

  What level of force is appropriate?

  ♦ Is retreat possible?   _____ Yes   _____ No

Based on the scenario and the elements of force, what level of force on the use of force continuum is reasonable and necessary?

> _ Presence
>
> _ Verbal
>
> _ Empty Hand / Personal Weapons
>
> _ OC Spray
>
> _ Impact Weapon / Weapon of Opportunity
>
> _ Lethal Force

Notes: _____

_____

_____

_____

_____

_____

_____

_____

_____

_____

_____

_____

_____

_____

_____

_____

_____

_____

<u>Scenario #28: Off-Duty Contact</u>

You are off duty with your spouse enjoying a date night at a club. An offender on your caseload walks up to you with a bottle of beer in his hand and says, "*I will be keeping an eye on you and yours all night.*" He then says, "*We can talk more outside and it won't be with words.*"

What do you do?

<u>Elements of Force:</u>

<u>Ability</u> - an attacker possesses the power to injure or kill. This power may come in the form of a weapon (gun, knife, club, etc.) or through disparity of force.

♦   Does the subject have <u>ability</u> to do harm to you as the officer or to a third party?

_____ Yes   _____ No

<u>Opportunity</u> - an attacker is capable of immediately employing the power to injure or kill. Two components to opportunity are distance and obstacles.

♦   Does the subject have <u>opportunity</u> to do harm to you as the officer or to a third party?

_____ Yes   _____ No

<u>Jeopardy</u> - an attacker is acting in such a manner that a reasonable and prudent person would conclude he/she intends to injure or kill.

♦   Are you or a third party in jeopardy? _____ Yes   _____ No

<u>Preclusion</u> - officer assessment to determine if a lower level of force would be appropriate or ineffective; and retreat is not possible.

What level of force is appropriate?

♦   Is retreat possible?   _____ Yes   _____ No

Based on the scenario and the elements of force, what level of force on the use of force continuum is reasonable and necessary?

      _ Presence

      _ Verbal

      _ Empty Hand / Personal Weapons

      _ OC Spray

      _ Impact Weapon / Weapon of Opportunity

      _ Lethal Force

Notes: _____

_____

_____

_____

_____

_____

_____

_____

_____

_____

_____

_____

_____

_____

_____

_____

_____

Scenario #29: The Expectations of Parole

You are in an interview room with a new parolee reviewing the terms of parolee and a behavior contract. The parolee says that you are setting him up to fail. You explain that these are common requirements with all parolees and that he has the same expectations. The parolee gets very mad and slams both hands on the table yelling, *"You might as well put me back in prison! I can't do this after being locked up for so long. Fuck you."*

What do you do?

Elements of Force:

Ability - an attacker possesses the power to injure or kill. This power may come in the form of a weapon (gun, knife, club, etc.) or through disparity of force.

- Does the subject have <u>ability</u> to do harm to you as the officer or to a third party?

    ____ Yes   ____ No

Opportunity - an attacker is capable of immediately employing the power to injure or kill. Two components to opportunity are distance and obstacles.

- Does the subject have <u>opportunity</u> to do harm to you as the officer or to a third party?

    ____ Yes   ____ No

Jeopardy - an attacker is acting in such a manner that a reasonable and prudent person would conclude he/she intends to injure or kill.

- Are you or a third party in jeopardy? ____ Yes   ____ No

Preclusion - officer assessment to determine if a lower level of force would be appropriate or ineffective; and retreat is not possible.

What level of force is appropriate?

- Is retreat possible?   ____ Yes   ____ No

Based on the scenario and the elements of force, what level of force on the use of force continuum is reasonable and necessary?

     _ Presence

     _ Verbal

     _ Empty Hand / Personal Weapons

     _ OC Spray

     _ Impact Weapon / Weapon of Opportunity

     _ Lethal Force

Notes: _____

_____

_____

_____

_____

_____

_____

_____

_____

_____

_____

_____

_____

_____

_____

_____

_____

Scenario #30: Juvenile Home Contact with Abusive Stepfather

You are conducting a home contact with a juvenile at his mother's home. The mother is recently remarried and the stepfather and juvenile do not get along. In the past the juvenile has confided in you that the stepfather is an abusive alcoholic who hates authority. When you arrive the juvenile and stepfather are home but the mother is still at work. As you are talking to the juvenile the stepfather starts talking about the time he was on probation and all PO's are, "*power hungry little bitches with a badge.*" You immediately sense that the stepfather is intoxicated and becoming aggressive toward you. He aggressively walks to you and firmly grabs your arm stating, "*get the hell out of my house.*" He aggressively shoves you toward the door. The juvenile is yelling at the stepfather to stop but instead the stepfather begins punching the juvenile in the face.

What do you do?

Elements of Force:

Ability - an attacker possesses the power to injure or kill. This power may come in the form of a weapon (gun, knife, club, etc.) or through disparity of force.

- ♦ Does the subject have <u>ability</u> to do harm to you as the officer or to a third party?

    _____ Yes   _____ No

Opportunity - an attacker is capable of immediately employing the power to injure or kill. Two components to opportunity are distance and obstacles.

- ♦ Does the subject have <u>opportunity</u> to do harm to you as the officer or to a third party?

    _____ Yes   _____ No

Jeopardy - an attacker is acting in such a manner that a reasonable and prudent person would conclude he/she intends to injure or kill.

- ♦ Are you or a third party in jeopardy? _____ Yes   _____ No

Preclusion - officer assessment to determine if a lower level of force would be appropriate or ineffective; and retreat is not possible.

What level of force is appropriate?

♦ Is retreat possible? ____ Yes ____ No

Based on the scenario and the elements of force, what level of force on the use of force continuum is reasonable and necessary?

_ Presence

_ Verbal

_ Empty Hand / Personal Weapons

_ OC Spray

_ Impact Weapon / Weapon of Opportunity

_ Lethal Force

Notes: _____

_____

_____

_____

_____

_____

_____

_____

_____

_____

_____

_____

_____

_____

_____

_____

_____

Scenario #31: Unscheduled Home Contact

You are conducting an unscheduled home contact on an adult offender on parole. The offender lives in a residence that has a 20 foot walkway to the front door. As you get about half way to the front door the offender opens the door, aims a shotgun and begins to shoot at you.

What do you do?

Elements of Force:

Ability - an attacker possesses the power to injure or kill. This power may come in the form of a weapon (gun, knife, club, etc.) or through disparity of force.

- Does the subject have <u>ability</u> to do harm to you as the officer or to a third party?

    ____ Yes   ____ No

Opportunity - an attacker is capable of immediately employing the power to injure or kill. Two components to opportunity are distance and obstacles.

- Does the subject have <u>opportunity</u> to do harm to you as the officer or to a third party?

    ____ Yes   ____ No

Jeopardy - an attacker is acting in such a manner that a reasonable and prudent person would conclude he/she intends to injure or kill.

- Are you or a third party in jeopardy? ____ Yes   ____ No

Preclusion - officer assessment to determine if a lower level of force would be appropriate or ineffective; and retreat is not possible.

What level of force is appropriate?

- Is retreat possible?   ____ Yes   ____ No

Based on the scenario and the elements of force, what level of force on the use of force continuum is reasonable and necessary?

_ Presence

_ Verbal

_ Empty Hand / Personal Weapons

_ OC Spray

_ Impact Weapon / Weapon of Opportunity

_ Lethal Force

Notes: _____

_____

_____

_____

_____

_____

_____

_____

_____

_____

_____

_____

_____

_____

_____

_____

_____

_____

Scenario #32: Danger in the Kitchen

You are conducting an unscheduled home contact on an adult female offender who lives alone and is on probation for aggravated assault. It is 5:30PM and the offender is cooking dinner. The offender says she needs to season her steak and calmly heads toward the kitchen. You stay in the dining room area which is about 12 feet from the kitchen. The offender seasons the steak and then turns away from you to reach for something that you cannot see. The offender turns around with a butcher knife in her hand and aggressively attacks you.

What do you do?

Elements of Force:

Ability - an attacker possesses the power to injure or kill. This power may come in the form of a weapon (gun, knife, club, etc.) or through disparity of force.

- ◆ Does the subject have <u>ability</u> to do harm to you as the officer or to a third party?

    ____ Yes   ____ No

Opportunity - an attacker is capable of immediately employing the power to injure or kill. Two components to opportunity are distance and obstacles.

- ◆ Does the subject have <u>opportunity</u> to do harm to you as the officer or to a third party?

    ____ Yes   ____ No

Jeopardy - an attacker is acting in such a manner that a reasonable and prudent person would conclude he/she intends to injure or kill.

- ◆ Are you or a third party in jeopardy? ____ Yes   ____ No

Preclusion - officer assessment to determine if a lower level of force would be appropriate or ineffective; and retreat is not possible.

    What level of force is appropriate?

- ◆ Is retreat possible?   ____ Yes   ____ No

Based on the scenario and the elements of force, what level of force on the use of force continuum is reasonable and necessary?

_ Presence

_ Verbal

_ Empty Hand / Personal Weapons

_ OC Spray

_ Impact Weapon / Weapon of Opportunity

_ Lethal Force

Notes: _____

_____

_____

_____

_____

_____

_____

_____

_____

_____

_____

_____

_____

_____

_____

_____

_____

_____

_____

Scenario #33: Suicidal Juvenile

A 17 year old male has reported to the probation office for his scheduled contact. You can tell by his demeanor that something is not normal. He appears very quiet and withdrawn. You both take a seat and you ask him what is going on. He responds, *"My life is falling apart. My parents hate me, my girlfriend broke up with me and my friends all want me to do things that I should not be doing. I can't handle the pressure anymore."* As you begin to offer some suggestions he begins to cry. He then reaches in his pocket and pulls out a pocket knife, opens it and starts to cut his neck and stab his abdomen. The blood from his neck is spurting everywhere.

What do you do?

Elements of Force:

Ability - an attacker possesses the power to injure or kill. This power may come in the form of a weapon (gun, knife, club, etc.) or through disparity of force.

- ♦ Does the subject have <u>ability</u> to do harm to you as the officer or to a third party?

   _____ Yes   _____ No

Opportunity - an attacker is capable of immediately employing the power to injure or kill. Two components to opportunity are distance and obstacles.

- ♦ Does the subject have <u>opportunity</u> to do harm to you as the officer or to a third party?

   _____ Yes   _____ No

Jeopardy - an attacker is acting in such a manner that a reasonable and prudent person would conclude he/she intends to injure or kill.

- ♦ Are you or a third party in jeopardy? _____ Yes   _____ No

Preclusion - officer assessment to determine if a lower level of force would be appropriate or ineffective; and retreat is not possible.

   What level of force is appropriate?

- ♦ Is retreat possible? ____ Yes ____ No

Based on the scenario and the elements of force, what level of force on the use of force continuum is reasonable and necessary?

- _ Presence
- _ Verbal
- _ Empty Hand / Personal Weapons
- _ OC Spray
- _ Impact Weapon / Weapon of Opportunity
- _ Lethal Force

Notes: _____

_____

_____

Scenario #34: Name Calling

You conduct a random home contact to a 15 year old female who is on your caseload for shoplifting, assault and resisting arrest. She has successfully completed all treatment and has been doing very well. At the home is the juvenile and three of her girlfriends. You are invited inside the house when two of the friends start to verbally harass you. The offender tells them to stop but the girls continue to verbally berate you by calling you a *"pig, bitch, and tramp."* The juvenile offender is trying to get the girls to stop calling you names but they keep doing it anyway.

What do you do?

Elements of Force:

Ability - an attacker possesses the power to injure or kill. This power may come in the form of a weapon (gun, knife, club, etc.) or through disparity of force.

- ♦ Does the subject have <u>ability</u> to do harm to you as the officer or to a third party?

    _____ Yes   _____ No

Opportunity - an attacker is capable of immediately employing the power to injure or kill. Two components to opportunity are distance and obstacles.

- ♦ Does the subject have <u>opportunity</u> to do harm to you as the officer or to a third party?

    _____ Yes   _____ No

Jeopardy - an attacker is acting in such a manner that a reasonable and prudent person would conclude he/she intends to injure or kill.

- ♦ Are you or a third party in jeopardy? _____ Yes   _____ No

Preclusion - officer assessment to determine if a lower level of force would be appropriate or ineffective; and retreat is not possible.

    What level of force is appropriate?

- ♦ Is retreat possible?   _____ Yes   _____ No

Based on the scenario and the elements of force, what level of force on the use of force continuum is reasonable and necessary?

_ Presence

_ Verbal

_ Empty Hand / Personal Weapons

_ OC Spray

_ Impact Weapon / Weapon of Opportunity

_ Lethal Force

Notes: _____

_____

_____

_____

_____

_____

_____

_____

_____

_____

_____

_____

_____

_____

_____

_____

_____

_____

Scenario #35: Absconder

You are assigned to the Fugitive Apprehension Unit (Warrants Unit) to find and arrest absconders. You get an anonymous tip that a parolee you are looking for is at his girlfriend's house. You conduct surveillance on the house and with the use of binoculars you can see him in the living room. You call the local police department for backup. The police surround the house while you and two officers approach the front door. When you knock the girlfriend answers the door and immediately yells, "It's the police." The offender barricades himself in the bathroom. The police interview the girlfriend who tells the officers that he has a gun with him and that he is crazy.

What do you do?

Elements of Force:

Ability - an attacker possesses the power to injure or kill. This power may come in the form of a weapon (gun, knife, club, etc.) or through disparity of force.

   ♦   Does the subject have <u>ability</u> to do harm to you as the officer or to a third party?

　　　_____ Yes 　　　　_____ No

Opportunity - an attacker is capable of immediately employing the power to injure or kill. Two components to opportunity are distance and obstacles.

   ♦   Does the subject have <u>opportunity</u> to do harm to you as the officer or to a third party?

　　　_____ Yes 　　　　_____ No

Jeopardy - an attacker is acting in such a manner that a reasonable and prudent person would conclude he/she intends to injure or kill.

   ♦   Are you or a third party in jeopardy? _____ Yes 　　　　_____ No

Preclusion - officer assessment to determine if a lower level of force would be appropriate or ineffective; and retreat is not possible.

　　　What level of force is appropriate?

♦ Is retreat possible? _____ Yes _____ No

Based on the scenario and the elements of force, what level of force on the use of force continuum is reasonable and necessary?

_ Presence

_ Verbal

_ Empty Hand / Personal Weapons

_ OC Spray

_ Impact Weapon / Weapon of Opportunity

_ Lethal Force

Notes: _____

_____

_____

_____

_____

_____

_____

_____

_____

_____

_____

_____

_____

_____

_____

_____

_____

Scenario #36: U.S. Marshals Fugitive Task Force

You are assigned to your probation departments Fugitive Apprehension Unit. You have also been assigned to work with the U.S. Marshals Fugitive Task Force. Today, you and the Marshals are looking for a convicted murderer who committed a triple homicide. You are in the back seat of the Marshals vehicle with three U.S. Marshals. You are following a car that the murderer is driving. The Marshals notify local police that they plan on doing a vehicle stop. When the Marshals turn on their lights and sirens the vehicle runs. The Marshals give chase and the suspect vehicle crashes in the middle of an intersection. Your vehicle is right behind the suspect vehicle. The suspect exist the car and immediately begins firing his handgun at your vehicle.

What do you do?

Elements of Force:

Ability - an attacker possesses the power to injure or kill. This power may come in the form of a weapon (gun, knife, club, etc.) or through disparity of force.

♦ Does the subject have <u>ability</u> to do harm to you as the officer or to a third party?

_____ Yes   _____ No

Opportunity - an attacker is capable of immediately employing the power to injure or kill. Two components to opportunity are distance and obstacles.

♦ Does the subject have <u>opportunity</u> to do harm to you as the officer or to a third party?

_____ Yes   _____ No

Jeopardy - an attacker is acting in such a manner that a reasonable and prudent person would conclude he/she intends to injure or kill.

♦ Are you or a third party in jeopardy? _____ Yes   _____ No

Preclusion - officer assessment to determine if a lower level of force would be appropriate or ineffective; and retreat is not possible.

What level of force is appropriate?

♦   Is retreat possible?   _____ Yes   _____ No

Based on the scenario and the elements of force, what level of force on the use of force continuum is reasonable and necessary?

_ Presence

_ Verbal

_ Empty Hand / Personal Weapons

_ OC Spray

_ Impact Weapon / Weapon of Opportunity

_ Lethal Force

Notes: _____

_____

_____

_____

_____

_____

_____

_____

_____

_____

_____

_____

_____

_____

_____

_____

Scenario #37: In Office Arrest - Domestic Violence

A domestic violence offender is reporting to the office today and you plan on arresting the offender for violating numerous rules such as drinking alcohol and having multiple unapproved contacts with the victim. The offender does not know that he is going to be arrested. You properly escort the offender to the interview room where he promptly sits down. You immediately inform him that his is under arrest for violating probation and that he needs to stand up. He defiantly looks at you, crosses his arms, and states, "*you are not arresting me, I did nothing wrong.*" You give him another verbal command to stand up and turn around. The offender just sits there and refuses to comply.

What do you do?

<u>Elements of Force:</u>

<u>Ability</u> - an attacker possesses the power to injure or kill. This power may come in the form of a weapon (gun, knife, club, etc.) or through disparity of force.

- ♦ Does the subject have <u>ability</u> to do harm to you as the officer or to a third party?

    _____ Yes   _____ No

<u>Opportunity</u> - an attacker is capable of immediately employing the power to injure or kill. Two components to opportunity are distance and obstacles.

- ♦ Does the subject have <u>opportunity</u> to do harm to you as the officer or to a third party?

    _____ Yes   _____ No

<u>Jeopardy</u> - an attacker is acting in such a manner that a reasonable and prudent person would conclude he/she intends to injure or kill.

- ♦ Are you or a third party in jeopardy? _____ Yes   _____ No

<u>Preclusion</u> - officer assessment to determine if a lower level of force would be appropriate or ineffective; and retreat is not possible.

    What level of force is appropriate?

♦   Is retreat possible?   ____ Yes   ____ No

Based on the scenario and the elements of force, what level of force on the use of force continuum is reasonable and necessary?

_ Presence

_ Verbal

_ Empty Hand / Personal Weapons

_ OC Spray

_ Impact Weapon / Weapon of Opportunity

_ Lethal Force

Notes: _____

_____

_____

_____

_____

_____

_____

_____

_____

_____

_____

_____

_____

_____

_____

_____

_____

_____

<u>Scenario #38: What To Do?</u>

You are conducting an unscheduled home contact on a juvenile offender. It is 7:12PM and as you approach the residence you stop to listen and observe. You hear a loud verbal altercation coming from inside of the residence. You hear what sounds like glass breaking and a female screaming. Clearly there is a very tense argument between a man and a women in the residence. You decide not to knock on the door because of safety concerns.

What do you do?

<u>**Elements of Force:**</u>

<u>**Ability**</u> - an attacker possesses the power to injure or kill. This power may come in the form of a weapon (gun, knife, club, etc.) or through disparity of force.

- ♦ Does the subject have <u>ability</u> to do harm to you as the officer or to a third party?

    _____ Yes   _____ No

<u>**Opportunity**</u> - an attacker is capable of immediately employing the power to injure or kill. Two components to opportunity are distance and obstacles.

- ♦ Does the subject have <u>opportunity</u> to do harm to you as the officer or to a third party?

    _____ Yes   _____ No

<u>**Jeopardy**</u> - an attacker is acting in such a manner that a reasonable and prudent person would conclude he/she intends to injure or kill.

- ♦ Are you or a third party in jeopardy? _____ Yes   _____ No

<u>**Preclusion**</u> - officer assessment to determine if a lower level of force would be appropriate or ineffective; and retreat is not possible.

    What level of force is appropriate?

- ♦ Is retreat possible?   _____ Yes   _____ No

Scott Kirshner

Based on the scenario and the elements of force, what level of force on the use of force continuum is reasonable and necessary?

_ Presence

_ Verbal

_ Empty Hand / Personal Weapons

_ OC Spray

_ Impact Weapon / Weapon of Opportunity

_ Lethal Force

Notes: _____

_____

_____

_____

_____

_____

_____

_____

_____

_____

_____

_____

_____

_____

_____

_____

_____

_____

Scenario #39: Out of Control Mother

You are conducting a home contact on a 16 year old male who lives with his divorced mother. Each of you are sitting in the living room discussing the progress of the juvenile. The mother begins to yell at you stating, *"He is out of control and you don't do a damn thing to keep him in line. What the hell good is probation if you don't do anything!"* The mother then slaps the juvenile in the face calling him, *"a worthless piece of shit."* The mother then stands up and says she should slap you because you are also worthless. She begins to aggressively walk toward you.

What do you do?

Elements of Force:

Ability - an attacker possesses the power to injure or kill. This power may come in the form of a weapon (gun, knife, club, etc.) or through disparity of force.

- ♦ Does the subject have <u>ability</u> to do harm to you as the officer or to a third party?

   ____ Yes   ____ No

Opportunity - an attacker is capable of immediately employing the power to injure or kill. Two components to opportunity are distance and obstacles.

- ♦ Does the subject have <u>opportunity</u> to do harm to you as the officer or to a third party?

   ____ Yes   ____ No

Jeopardy - an attacker is acting in such a manner that a reasonable and prudent person would conclude he/she intends to injure or kill.

- ♦ Are you or a third party in jeopardy? ____ Yes   ____ No

Preclusion - officer assessment to determine if a lower level of force would be appropriate or ineffective; and retreat is not possible.

   What level of force is appropriate?

- ♦ Is retreat possible?   ____ Yes   ____ No

Based on the scenario and the elements of force, what level of force on the use of force continuum is reasonable and necessary?

_ Presence

_ Verbal

_ Empty Hand / Personal Weapons

_ OC Spray

_ Impact Weapon / Weapon of Opportunity

_ Lethal Force

Notes: _____

_____

_____

_____

_____

_____

_____

_____

_____

_____

_____

_____

_____

_____

_____

_____

_____

_____

_____

<u>Scenario #40: Basketball</u>

You and your partner are working a juvenile caseload. Tonight you decide to visit a local park where some of the juvenile offenders like to play basketball. You park your car in the distance and use binoculars to see that many of the juveniles appear to be drinking alcohol. You decide to approach the group of 10 juveniles since 3 of them are on your caseloads. As you get closer they notice you walking up. All of the kids are polite and respectful. When you ask the juveniles on your caseload if they have been drinking they say, "*no.*" You then ask them to do a breathalyzer. All of the juveniles become agitated and say you have no right to do that. Some of the juveniles say they are not on probation and won't do it. You respond that you only want to breathalyze the three juveniles who are on probation. All of a sudden the group becomes verbally aggressive and tells you to "*move on right now we ain't playing this game.*"

What do you do?

<u>Elements of Force:</u>

<u>Ability</u> - an attacker possesses the power to injure or kill. This power may come in the form of a weapon (gun, knife, club, etc.) or through disparity of force.

- ♦ Does the subject have <u>ability</u> to do harm to you as the officer or to a third party?

    _____ Yes   _____ No

<u>Opportunity</u> - an attacker is capable of immediately employing the power to injure or kill. Two components to opportunity are distance and obstacles.

- ♦ Does the subject have <u>opportunity</u> to do harm to you as the officer or to a third party?

    _____ Yes   _____ No

<u>Jeopardy</u> - an attacker is acting in such a manner that a reasonable and prudent person would conclude he/she intends to injure or kill.

- ♦ Are you or a third party in jeopardy? _____ Yes   _____ No

Preclusion - officer assessment to determine if a lower level of force would be appropriate or ineffective; and retreat is not possible.

What level of force is appropriate?

♦ Is retreat possible? _____ Yes _____ No

Based on the scenario and the elements of force, what level of force on the use of force continuum is reasonable and necessary?

_ Presence

_ Verbal

_ Empty Hand / Personal Weapons

_ OC Spray

_ Impact Weapon / Weapon of Opportunity

_ Lethal Force

Notes: _____

_____

_____

_____

_____

_____

_____

_____

_____

_____

_____

_____

_____

_____

_____

Scenario #41: Arrest

You and two partners are going to an adult offenders place of employment to arrest him on an active warrant. The offender knows he has a warrant but will not turn himself in despite being given the opportunity to clear up the warrant. The offender works as a motorcycle mechanic at a local biker shop. When you arrive the offender is working on a motorcycle. You inform him that he is under arrest for violating probation and you handcuff him without incident. The other officers are using the contact/cover principle. As you are escorting the offender to the vehicle to transport him to jail his boss rushes over and angrily asks, *"What the hell are you doing? He is my best mechanic. I need him."* The boss then grabs you by the arm and demands that you let him go right now. At this point five big bikers and the boss are confronting the three of you stating that you are not leaving with their worker.

What do you do?

Elements of Force:

Ability - an attacker possesses the power to injure or kill. This power may come in the form of a weapon (gun, knife, club, etc.) or through disparity of force.

- ♦ Does the subject have <u>ability</u> to do harm to you as the officer or to a third party?

  _____ Yes   _____ No

Opportunity - an attacker is capable of immediately employing the power to injure or kill. Two components to opportunity are distance and obstacles.

- ♦ Does the subject have <u>opportunity</u> to do harm to you as the officer or to a third party?

  _____ Yes   _____ No

Jeopardy - an attacker is acting in such a manner that a reasonable and prudent person would conclude he/she intends to injure or kill.

- ♦ Are you or a third party in jeopardy? _____ Yes   _____ No

Preclusion - officer assessment to determine if a lower level of force would be appropriate or ineffective; and retreat is not possible.

What level of force is appropriate?

♦ Is retreat possible? ____ Yes ____ No

Based on the scenario and the elements of force, what level of force on the use of force continuum is reasonable and necessary?

_ Presence

_ Verbal

_ Empty Hand / Personal Weapons

_ OC Spray

_ Impact Weapon / Weapon of Opportunity

_ Lethal Force

Notes: _____

_____

_____

_____

_____

_____

_____

_____

_____

_____

_____

_____

_____

_____

_____

Scenario #42: Early to Work

You arrive at 7:00AM to the parole office to catch up on paperwork and prepare for office day. The office does not open until 8:00AM. After you park your personal vehicle you start walking toward the employee entrance. As you get closer you notice two individuals you have never seen before this morning. As you get within about 15 yards both men turn their attention toward you. There is no one else in the parking lot. You ask if they need help when one of the men says, "*that's him*." They both start sprinting toward you.

What do you do?

Elements of Force:

Ability - an attacker possesses the power to injure or kill. This power may come in the form of a weapon (gun, knife, club, etc.) or through disparity of force.

- ♦ Does the subject have <u>ability</u> to do harm to you as the officer or to a third party?

    ____ Yes   ____ No

Opportunity - an attacker is capable of immediately employing the power to injure or kill. Two components to opportunity are distance and obstacles.

- ♦ Does the subject have <u>opportunity</u> to do harm to you as the officer or to a third party?

    ____ Yes   ____ No

Jeopardy - an attacker is acting in such a manner that a reasonable and prudent person would conclude he/she intends to injure or kill.

- ♦ Are you or a third party in jeopardy? ____ Yes   ____ No

Preclusion - officer assessment to determine if a lower level of force would be appropriate or ineffective; and retreat is not possible.

    What level of force is appropriate?

- ♦ Is retreat possible?   ____ Yes   ____ No

Based on the scenario and the elements of force, what level of force on the use of force continuum is reasonable and necessary?

_ Presence

_ Verbal

_ Empty Hand / Personal Weapons

_ OC Spray

_ Impact Weapon / Weapon of Opportunity

_ Lethal Force

Notes: _____

_____

_____

_____

_____

_____

_____

_____

_____

_____

_____

_____

_____

_____

_____

_____

_____

_____

_____

Scenario #43: Tailgating

You are conducting field contacts in your personal vehicle. After your last offender contact you think a vehicle is following you. To be cautious you change lanes numerous times but the vehicle is still within sight. You decide to stop at a gas station to get a drink. After you leave the store you notice the vehicle is parked at a gas pump but the occupant never got out of his vehicle. You get back on the road and now notice that the vehicle is tailgating you. There is no doubt that you are being followed by an unknown individual.

What do you do?

Elements of Force:

Ability - an attacker possesses the power to injure or kill. This power may come in the form of a weapon (gun, knife, club, etc.) or through disparity of force.

- ◆ Does the subject have <u>ability</u> to do harm to you as the officer or to a third party?

    _____ Yes   _____ No

Opportunity - an attacker is capable of immediately employing the power to injure or kill. Two components to opportunity are distance and obstacles.

- ◆ Does the subject have <u>opportunity</u> to do harm to you as the officer or to a third party?

    _____ Yes   _____ No

Jeopardy - an attacker is acting in such a manner that a reasonable and prudent person would conclude he/she intends to injure or kill.

- ◆ Are you or a third party in jeopardy? _____ Yes   _____ No

Preclusion - officer assessment to determine if a lower level of force would be appropriate or ineffective; and retreat is not possible.

    What level of force is appropriate?

- ◆ Is retreat possible?   _____ Yes   _____ No

Based on the scenario and the elements of force, what level of force on the use of force continuum is reasonable and necessary?

    _ Presence

    _ Verbal

    _ Empty Hand / Personal Weapons

    _ OC Spray

    _ Impact Weapon / Weapon of Opportunity

    _ Lethal Force

Notes: _____

_____

_____

_____

_____

_____

_____

_____

_____

_____

_____

_____

_____

_____

_____

_____

_____

_____

Scenario #44: Reach Out and Touch You

You recently arrested a probationer who is part of a criminal syndicate. The day you arrested him he clearly stated, "*This is not over and I will reach out and touch you.*" About a week later you start getting a lot of hang up calls on your personal cell phone. One night you notice a vehicle that keeps passing by your house. The next night a rock is thrown through your front window and your vehicles tires are slashed.

What do you do?

Elements of Force:

Ability - an attacker possesses the power to injure or kill. This power may come in the form of a weapon (gun, knife, club, etc.) or through disparity of force.

♦   Does the subject have <u>ability</u> to do harm to you as the officer or to a third party?

_____ Yes   _____ No

Opportunity - an attacker is capable of immediately employing the power to injure or kill. Two components to opportunity are distance and obstacles.

♦   Does the subject have <u>opportunity</u> to do harm to you as the officer or to a third party?

_____ Yes   _____ No

Jeopardy - an attacker is acting in such a manner that a reasonable and prudent person would conclude he/she intends to injure or kill.

♦   Are you or a third party in jeopardy? _____ Yes   _____ No

Preclusion - officer assessment to determine if a lower level of force would be appropriate or ineffective; and retreat is not possible.

What level of force is appropriate?

♦   Is retreat possible?   _____ Yes   _____ No

Based on the scenario and the elements of force, what level of force on the use of force continuum is reasonable and necessary?

     _ Presence

     _ Verbal

     _ Empty Hand / Personal Weapons

     _ OC Spray

     _ Impact Weapon / Weapon of Opportunity

     _ Lethal Force

Notes: _____

_____

_____

_____

_____

_____

_____

_____

_____

_____

_____

_____

_____

_____

_____

_____

Officer Survival Training Scenarios

Scenario #45: Fire Alarm…Again!

It is office day and you are seeing a steady stream of offenders. While finishing up some paperwork from your last contact the fire alarm goes off. This is the third week in a row that it has gone off and most people are now immune to the alarm. The office supervisors are mandating all staff to immediately evacuate to the predetermined location. An employee reports to a supervisor that there are two unattended backpacks in the evacuation area. Within 5 seconds both backpacks explode simultaneously. You are not injured.

What do you do?

Elements of Force:

Ability - an attacker possesses the power to injure or kill. This power may come in the form of a weapon (gun, knife, club, etc.) or through disparity of force.

♦ Does the subject have <u>ability</u> to do harm to you as the officer or to a third party?

_____ Yes   _____ No

Opportunity - an attacker is capable of immediately employing the power to injure or kill. Two components to opportunity are distance and obstacles.

♦ Does the subject have <u>opportunity</u> to do harm to you as the officer or to a third party?

_____ Yes   _____ No

Jeopardy - an attacker is acting in such a manner that a reasonable and prudent person would conclude he/she intends to injure or kill.

♦ Are you or a third party in jeopardy? _____ Yes   _____ No

Preclusion - officer assessment to determine if a lower level of force would be appropriate or ineffective; and retreat is not possible.

What level of force is appropriate?

♦ Is retreat possible?   _____ Yes   _____ No

Based on the scenario and the elements of force, what level of force on the use of force continuum is reasonable and necessary?

_ Presence

_ Verbal

_ Empty Hand / Personal Weapons

_ OC Spray

_ Impact Weapon / Weapon of Opportunity

_ Lethal Force

Notes: _____

_____

_____

_____

_____

_____

_____

_____

_____

_____

_____

_____

_____

_____

_____

_____

_____

_____

Scenario #46: Your Dead

Over the last week you have received numerous voicemails on your work cellphone saying, *"Your dead."* The call is from a blocked phone number so you do not know who is calling. When you answer the phone the caller just hangs up without saying anything. You report the incident to your supervisor and a police report is made regarding the incident. The phone messages randomly stopped so there was no way to find out who made the call. A month passes when you get a call from a blocked number. When you answer a male states, *"Today is the day you die...your dead."* The caller immediately hangs up and you do not recognize the voice.

What do you do?

Elements of Force:

Ability - an attacker possesses the power to injure or kill. This power may come in the form of a weapon (gun, knife, club, etc.) or through disparity of force.

- ♦ Does the subject have <u>ability</u> to do harm to you as the officer or to a third party?

    ____ Yes   ____ No

Opportunity - an attacker is capable of immediately employing the power to injure or kill. Two components to opportunity are distance and obstacles.

- ♦ Does the subject have <u>opportunity</u> to do harm to you as the officer or to a third party?

    ____ Yes   ____ No

Jeopardy - an attacker is acting in such a manner that a reasonable and prudent person would conclude he/she intends to injure or kill.

- ♦ Are you or a third party in jeopardy? ____ Yes   ____ No

Preclusion - officer assessment to determine if a lower level of force would be appropriate or ineffective; and retreat is not possible.

    What level of force is appropriate?

♦ Is retreat possible?   _____ Yes   _____ No

Based on the scenario and the elements of force, what level of force on the use of force continuum is reasonable and necessary?

_ Presence

_ Verbal

_ Empty Hand / Personal Weapons

_ OC Spray

_ Impact Weapon / Weapon of Opportunity

_ Lethal Force

Notes: _____

_____

_____

_____

_____

_____

_____

_____

_____

_____

_____

_____

_____

_____

_____

_____

_____

_____

Scenario #47: Set Up

You get a phone call from the ex-girlfriend of an offender who is on your caseload for domestic violence. She tells you she has information regarding the offender but she does not want to give it over the phone and she does not want to be seen at the probation office. She asks you to come by her house. She says it is important and that she is scared for her safety. It is toward the end of your work day so you decide to go over to the offenders ex-girlfriend's house and you will then head home after the contact. When you arrive at the ex-girlfriend's house she thanks you for coming over as she goes to sit on the couch. All of a sudden the offender is standing in the hall with a baseball bat angrily staring you down. You run to the front door to make a hasty exit. The front door opens but someone locked the security screen door from the outside. You are now locked inside of the house. Now, a second man that you do not know walks into the living room from the backyard door. He looks at you and says, *"I bet you didn't see this coming. How did you like the front door trick."*

What do you do?

Elements of Force:

Ability - an attacker possesses the power to injure or kill. This power may come in the form of a weapon (gun, knife, club, etc.) or through disparity of force.

- Does the subject have <u>ability</u> to do harm to you as the officer or to a third party?

  ____ Yes   ____ No

Opportunity - an attacker is capable of immediately employing the power to injure or kill. Two components to opportunity are distance and obstacles.

- Does the subject have <u>opportunity</u> to do harm to you as the officer or to a third party?

  ____ Yes   ____ No

Jeopardy - an attacker is acting in such a manner that a reasonable and prudent person would conclude he/she intends to injure or kill.

- ♦ Are you or a third party in jeopardy? ____ Yes   ____ No

Preclusion - officer assessment to determine if a lower level of force would be appropriate or ineffective; and retreat is not possible.

What level of force is appropriate?

- ♦ Is retreat possible?   ____ Yes   ____ No

Based on the scenario and the elements of force, what level of force on the use of force continuum is reasonable and necessary?

_ Presence

_ Verbal

_ Empty Hand / Personal Weapons

_ OC Spray

_ Impact Weapon / Weapon of Opportunity

_ Lethal Force

Notes: _____

_____

_____

_____

_____

_____

_____

_____

_____

_____

_____

_____

Scenario #48: Institutionalized

You are conducting contact at a halfway house with an offender who has been on parole for 8 months. The offender served 28 years in prison for murder and aggravated assault. During his time in prison he had very little disciplinary action which were all minor. He was well behaved as far as inmates go. At the halfway house he tells you that he is really struggling with life on the outside. He states that he is too stressed with rent, bills, people, freedom and life in general. You provide some options to help him cope but he tells you he just wants to go back to prison. He states he is institutionalized and that is where he feels comfortable and where he belongs. He says he is sorry but he is going to hurt you so that he gets sent back to prison. Before you can even respond he is physically attacking you with his hands and feet.

What do you do?

Elements of Force:

Ability - an attacker possesses the power to injure or kill. This power may come in the form of a weapon (gun, knife, club, etc.) or through disparity of force.

- ♦ Does the subject have <u>ability</u> to do harm to you as the officer or to a third party?

    ____ Yes   ____ No

Opportunity - an attacker is capable of immediately employing the power to injure or kill. Two components to opportunity are distance and obstacles.

- ♦ Does the subject have <u>opportunity</u> to do harm to you as the officer or to a third party?

    ____ Yes   ____ No

Jeopardy - an attacker is acting in such a manner that a reasonable and prudent person would conclude he/she intends to injure or kill.

- ♦ Are you or a third party in jeopardy? ____ Yes   ____ No

Preclusion - officer assessment to determine if a lower level of force would be appropriate or ineffective; and retreat is not possible.

> What level of force is appropriate?
>
> ♦ Is retreat possible?   ____ Yes   ____ No

Based on the scenario and the elements of force, what level of force on the use of force continuum is reasonable and necessary?

> _ Presence
>
> _ Verbal
>
> _ Empty Hand / Personal Weapons
>
> _ OC Spray
>
> _ Impact Weapon / Weapon of Opportunity
>
> _ Lethal Force

Notes: _____

_____

_____

_____

_____

_____

_____

_____

_____

_____

_____

_____

_____

_____

_____

_____

_____

<u>Scenario #49: Naughty Juvenile</u>

You receive a phone call from a mother of a juvenile sex offender that you are supervising. At the age of 13 the juvenile sexually assaulted a 7 year old neighbor girl. Now he is 16 years old and the mother thinks he has pornography in his bedroom. The mother states that her son will not let her in the room and he keeps the door locked all of the time. The mother asks you to come by and search the room when he gets home from school. You arrange a search team of 5 officers who are at the house when the juvenile gets home from school. When he walks in the house he knows something is up and starts to yell and scream at his mother. You calm him down and tell him to unlock the door to his bedroom so that it can be searched. The juvenile reluctantly agrees and gives you the key to the room. In the room you find pornographic magazines, DVD's and sex toys. The juvenile who was directed to sit at the dinner table becomes uncontrollably furious. He knocks the officer down who was standing by him and he then proceeds to throw drinking glasses at the other officers before running full speed to charge at officers in his bedroom with pure aggression and anger.

What do you do?

Elements of Force:

Ability - an attacker possesses the power to injure or kill. This power may come in the form of a weapon (gun, knife, club, etc.) or through disparity of force.

 ♦ Does the subject have <u>ability</u> to do harm to you as the officer or to a third party?

   ____ Yes   ____ No

Opportunity - an attacker is capable of immediately employing the power to injure or kill. Two components to opportunity are distance and obstacles.

 ♦ Does the subject have <u>opportunity</u> to do harm to you as the officer or to a third party?

   ____ Yes   ____ No

Jeopardy ·· an attacker is acting in such a manner that a reasonable and prudent person would conclude he/she intends to injure or kill.

◆   Are you or a third party in jeopardy? ____ Yes   ____ No

Preclusion - officer assessment to determine if a lower level of force would be appropriate or ineffective; and retreat is not possible.

What level of force is appropriate?

◆   Is retreat possible?   ____ Yes   ____ No

Based on the scenario and the elements of force, what level of force on the use of force continuum is reasonable and necessary?

_ Presence

_ Verbal

_ Empty Hand / Personal Weapons

_ OC Spray

_ Impact Weapon / Weapon of Opportunity

_ Lethal Force

Notes: _____

_____

_____

_____

_____

_____

_____

_____

_____

_____

_____

_____

<u>Scenario #50: Mental Illness</u>

You are conducting an office contact with an offender who was placed on probation for trespassing, stalking, and threatening. You have had multiple contacts with the offender who suffers from schizophrenia. The offender was described by his victim as very strange, crazy, and a lunatic who is potentially very dangerous. You are attempting to get him on a specialized Seriously Mentally Ill caseload so that he can obtain necessary services. During this contact you ask the offender how counseling is going to which he calmly replies, *"I could kill you. But, I could also eat your fingers."* You ask why he would say such a statement and he then responds that, *"Counseling is helping but they implanted me with a listening device that makes me say things I don't want to say."* You ask the offender how he feels right know? He replies, *"Your fingers would be tasty especially with urine. Actually, I really want to eat your 12 fingers."*

Clearly, you are not able to effectively communicate with this offender who is verbalizing irrational thoughts.

What do you do?

<u>Elements of Force:</u>

Ability - an attacker possesses the power to injure or kill. This power may come in the form of a weapon (gun, knife, club, etc.) or through disparity of force.

    ◆ Does the subject have <u>ability</u> to do harm to you as the officer or to a third party?

        ____ Yes   ____ No

Opportunity - an attacker is capable of immediately employing the power to injure or kill. Two components to opportunity are distance and obstacles.

    ◆ Does the subject have <u>opportunity</u> to do harm to you as the officer or to a third party?

        ____ Yes   ____ No

Jeopardy - an attacker is acting in such a manner that a reasonable and prudent person would conclude he/she intends to injure or kill.

- ♦ Are you or a third party in jeopardy? _____ Yes   _____ No

Preclusion - officer assessment to determine if a lower level of force would be appropriate or ineffective; and retreat is not possible.

What level of force is appropriate?

- ♦ Is retreat possible?   _____ Yes   _____ No

Based on the scenario and the elements of force, what level of force on the use of force continuum is reasonable and necessary?

_ Presence

_ Verbal

_ Empty Hand / Personal Weapons

_ OC Spray

_ Impact Weapon / Weapon of Opportunity

_ Lethal Force

Notes: _____

_____

_____

_____

_____

_____

_____

_____

_____

_____

_____

_____

<u>Scenario #51: Therapy Meeting</u>

You receive a phone call from a treatment counselor who states that an offender on your caseload is being disruptive in group class, misses classes, and has a negative attitude. The counselor requests a meeting with you, the offender and himself to discuss the offenders attitude about counseling. The meeting is held at the counselors office in a small room with a table and four chairs. The counselor explains to the offender that he needs to actively participate, attend all group classes and not be disruptive. The offender states that he does not need counseling and denies all the allegations being stated. The offender abruptly stands up and tells the counselor to "*fuck off.*" The offender then dives across the table and begins to violently choke the counselor.

What do you do?

<u>Elements of Force:</u>

<u>Ability</u> - an attacker possesses the power to injure or kill. This power may come in the form of a weapon (gun, knife, club, etc.) or through disparity of force.

- ♦ Does the subject have <u>ability</u> to do harm to you as the officer or to a third party?

    ____ Yes   ____ No

<u>Opportunity</u> - an attacker is capable of immediately employing the power to injure or kill. Two components to opportunity are distance and obstacles.

- ♦ Does the subject have <u>opportunity</u> to do harm to you as the officer or to a third party?

    ____ Yes   ____ No

<u>Jeopardy</u> - an attacker is acting in such a manner that a reasonable and prudent person would conclude he/she intends to injure or kill.

- ♦ Are you or a third party in jeopardy? ____ Yes   ____ No

<u>Preclusion</u> - officer assessment to determine if a lower level of force would be appropriate or ineffective; and retreat is not possible.

Scott Kirshner

What level of force is appropriate?

♦   Is retreat possible?   ____ Yes   ____ No

Based on the scenario and the elements of force, what level of force on the use of force continuum is reasonable and necessary?

_ Presence

_ Verbal

_ Empty Hand / Personal Weapons

_ OC Spray

_ Impact Weapon / Weapon of Opportunity

_ Lethal Force

Notes: _____

_____

_____

_____

_____

_____

_____

_____

_____

_____

_____

_____

_____

_____

_____

_____

_____

<u>Scenario #52: Sovereign Citizen</u>

You have a new offender assigned to your caseload that you are meeting for the first time to review terms and conditions of probation. The offender states to you that he is a "sovereign citizen" and he does not recognize your authority or the courts authority to place him on probation. He states that he will not sign any documents and if you force him to sign a document he will annotate it as "*signed under duress*." He also states that you do not have the right to come on his property or search any of his property. The offender states that if you violate his rights he has the right to defend himself as he sees fit.

What do you do?

<u>Elements of Force:</u>

<u>**Ability**</u> - an attacker possesses the power to injure or kill. This power may come in the form of a weapon (gun, knife, club, etc.) or through disparity of force.

- Does the subject have <u>ability</u> to do harm to you as the officer or to a third party?

    ____ Yes   ____ No

<u>**Opportunity**</u> - an attacker is capable of immediately employing the power to injure or kill. Two components to opportunity are distance and obstacles.

- Does the subject have <u>opportunity</u> to do harm to you as the officer or to a third party?

    ____ Yes   ____ No

<u>**Jeopardy**</u> - an attacker is acting in such a manner that a reasonable and prudent person would conclude he/she intends to injure or kill.

- Are you or a third party in jeopardy? ____ Yes   ____ No

<u>**Preclusion**</u> - officer assessment to determine if a lower level of force would be appropriate or ineffective; and retreat is not possible.

    What level of force is appropriate?

- Is retreat possible?   ____ Yes   ____ No

Based on the scenario and the elements of force, what level of force on the use of force continuum is reasonable and necessary?

    _ Presence

    _ Verbal

    _ Empty Hand / Personal Weapons

    _ OC Spray

    _ Impact Weapon / Weapon of Opportunity

    _ Lethal Force

Notes: _____

_____

_____

_____

_____

_____

_____

_____

_____

_____

_____

_____

_____

_____

_____

_____

_____

<u>Scenario #53: Office Stabbing</u>

You are conducting office day and just finished a contact with an offender. You are typing your notes into the computer when you hear a blood curling scream and someone yell, "*I've been stabbed.*" You cautiously exit your office and go down a hallway when you see a fellow officer lying on the ground holding his abdomen which is bleeding. An offender, holding a bloody knife in his hand begins to run toward your direction. You do not know if he is trying to escape or attack you.

What do you do?

Elements of Force:

Ability - an attacker possesses the power to injure or kill. This power may come in the form of a weapon (gun, knife, club, etc.) or through disparity of force.

- ◆ Does the subject have <u>ability</u> to do harm to you as the officer or to a third party?

    ____ Yes   ____ No

Opportunity - an attacker is capable of immediately employing the power to injure or kill. Two components to opportunity are distance and obstacles.

- ◆ Does the subject have <u>opportunity</u> to do harm to you as the officer or to a third party?

    ____ Yes   ____ No

Jeopardy - an attacker is acting in such a manner that a reasonable and prudent person would conclude he/she intends to injure or kill.

- ◆ Are you or a third party in jeopardy? ____ Yes   ____ No

Preclusion - officer assessment to determine if a lower level of force would be appropriate or ineffective; and retreat is not possible.

    What level of force is appropriate?

- ◆ Is retreat possible?   ____ Yes   ____ No

Based on the scenario and the elements of force, what level of force on the use of force continuum is reasonable and necessary?

      _ Presence

      _ Verbal

      _ Empty Hand / Personal Weapons

      _ OC Spray

      _ Impact Weapon / Weapon of Opportunity

      _ Lethal Force

Notes: _____

_____

_____

_____

_____

_____

_____

_____

_____

_____

_____

_____

_____

_____

_____

_____

_____

_____

Officer Survival Training Scenarios

Scenario #54: Group Fight

You are a juvenile probation officer who is facilitating a group of 12 juveniles on "Making Better Choices." You are facilitating this group with one other juvenile PO in a classroom at the probation office. After a 10 minute break you are resuming the class. A few of the juveniles are having words with each other and you provide a clear verbal command to stop and take your seats. Without warning a fight breaks out involving 8 of the juveniles. The other 4 juveniles do not participate in the fight and back away. Both you and your partner are giving loud, clear, and concise verbal commands to stop fighting. Despite excellent verbal commands the fight continues and some of the juveniles are now hitting the others with chairs.

What do you do?

Elements of Force:

Ability - an attacker possesses the power to injure or kill. This power may come in the form of a weapon (gun, knife, club, etc.) or through disparity of force.

- Does the subject have ability to do harm to you as the officer or to a third party?

____ Yes   ____ No

Opportunity - an attacker is capable of immediately employing the power to injure or kill. Two components to opportunity are distance and obstacles.

- Does the subject have opportunity to do harm to you as the officer or to a third party?

____ Yes   ____ No

Jeopardy - an attacker is acting in such a manner that a reasonable and prudent person would conclude he/she intends to injure or kill.

- Are you or a third party in jeopardy? ____ Yes   ____ No

Preclusion - officer assessment to determine if a lower level of force would be appropriate or ineffective; and retreat is not possible.

Scott Kirshner

What level of force is appropriate?   .

◆   Is retreat possible?   ____ Yes   ____ No

Based on the scenario and the elements of force, what level of force on the use of force continuum is reasonable and necessary?

_ Presence

_ Verbal

_ Empty Hand / Personal Weapons

_ OC Spray

_ Impact Weapon / Weapon of Opportunity

_ Lethal Force

Notes: _____

_____

_____

_____

_____

_____

_____

_____

_____

_____

_____

_____

_____

_____

_____

_____

_____

Scenario #55: Relapse

You are conducting office day and a parolee is in your office to discuss two positive drug tests for methamphetamine and his relapse. The parolee is attending treatment and his counselor says that he is actively participating but struggling with sobriety. As you discuss this situation with the parolee you are being calm, professional and supportive. The parole becomes verbally loud and yells at you stating, *"I'm trying my best to stay sober so stop riding my ass. I have attended all my treatment classes. I'm doing my best."* You tell the offender to calm down when he stands up points he index finger at you and yells, *"Fuck you."*

What do you do?

Elements of Force:

Ability - an attacker possesses the power to injure or kill. This power may come in the form of a weapon (gun, knife, club, etc.) or through disparity of force.

   ♦   Does the subject have ability to do harm to you as the officer or to a third party?

   _____ Yes   _____ No

Opportunity - an attacker is capable of immediately employing the power to injure or kill. Two components to opportunity are distance and obstacles.

   ♦   Does the subject have opportunity to do harm to you as the officer or to a third party?

   _____ Yes   _____ No

Jeopardy - an attacker is acting in such a manner that a reasonable and prudent person would conclude he/she intends to injure or kill.

   ♦   Are you or a third party in jeopardy? _____ Yes   _____ No

Preclusion - officer assessment to determine if a lower level of force would be appropriate or ineffective; and retreat is not possible.

   What level of force is appropriate?

- ♦ Is retreat possible? _____ Yes   _____ No

Based on the scenario and the elements of force, what level of force on the use of force continuum is reasonable and necessary?

_ Presence

_ Verbal

_ Empty Hand / Personal Weapons

_ OC Spray

_ Impact Weapon / Weapon of Opportunity

_ Lethal Force

Notes: _____

_____

_____

_____

_____

_____

_____

_____

_____

_____

_____

_____

_____

_____

_____

_____

_____

_____

_____

Scenario #56: Domestic Violence

You are conducting a field contact at an apartment complex. You knock on the offenders door but there is no answer. As you begin to walk back to your vehicle you pass an apartment that has the door halfway open. You hear a man and woman arguing. You slow down to listen when all of a sudden both come into view and you see the man violently hit the woman multiple times in her face with a closed fist. The man sees you and says, *"mind your own damn business"* and he then shuts the door. You hear the woman screaming for help.

What do you do?

Elements of Force:

Ability - an attacker possesses the power to injure or kill. This power may come in the form of a weapon (gun, knife, club, etc.) or through disparity of force.

- ♦ Does the subject have <u>ability</u> to do harm to you as the officer or to a third party?

    _____ Yes   _____ No

Opportunity - an attacker is capable of immediately employing the power to injure or kill. Two components to opportunity are distance and obstacles.

- ♦ Does the subject have <u>opportunity</u> to do harm to you as the officer or to a third party?

    _____ Yes   _____ No

Jeopardy - an attacker is acting in such a manner that a reasonable and prudent person would conclude he/she intends to injure or kill.

- ♦ Are you or a third party in jeopardy? _____ Yes   _____ No

Preclusion - officer assessment to determine if a lower level of force would be appropriate or ineffective; and retreat is not possible.

    What level of force is appropriate?

- ♦ Is retreat possible?   _____ Yes   _____ No

Scott Kirshner

Based on the scenario and the elements of force, what level of force on the use of force continuum is reasonable and necessary?

_ Presence

_ Verbal

_ Empty Hand / Personal Weapons

_ OC Spray

_ Impact Weapon / Weapon of Opportunity

_ Lethal Force

Notes: _____

_____

_____

_____

_____

_____

_____

_____

_____

_____

_____

_____

_____

_____

_____

_____

_____

_____

Scenario #57: Dog Attack

You are conducting a field contact at offenders home in a bad part of town. Many of the homeowners have dogs chained outside with no water or shelter. You have repeatedly called animal control to investigate. The residence you are contacting today is an offender who owns a dog. When you knock on the door the offender opens the front door and the dog immediately runs out of the house and attacks you by biting your leg.

What do you do?

Elements of Force:

Ability - an attacker possesses the power to injure or kill. This power may come in the form of a weapon (gun, knife, club, etc.) or through disparity of force.

 ♦ Does the subject have <u>ability</u> to do harm to you as the officer or to a third party?

 ____ Yes   ____ No

Opportunity - an attacker is capable of immediately employing the power to injure or kill. Two components to opportunity are distance and obstacles.

 ♦ Does the subject have <u>opportunity</u> to do harm to you as the officer or to a third party?

 ____ Yes   ____ No

Jeopardy - an attacker is acting in such a manner that a reasonable and prudent person would conclude he/she intends to injure or kill.

 ♦ Are you or a third party in jeopardy? ____ Yes   ____ No

Preclusion - officer assessment to determine if a lower level of force would be appropriate or ineffective; and retreat is not possible.

 What level of force is appropriate?

 ♦ Is retreat possible? ____ Yes   ____ No

Scott Kirshner

Based on the scenario and the elements of force, what level of force on the use of force continuum is reasonable and necessary?

_ Presence

_ Verbal

_ Empty Hand / Personal Weapons

_ OC Spray

_ Impact Weapon / Weapon of Opportunity

_ Lethal Force

Notes: _____

_____

_____

_____

_____

_____

_____

_____

_____

_____

_____

_____

_____

_____

_____

_____

_____

_____

Scenario #58: Drugged

You are conducting field work on a hot summer day. You typically drink a lot of water throughout the day and keep a lot of water bottles in your vehicle. Today, you forgot to bring extra water so you have not been drinking as much as normal to stay hydrated. You are conducting a residential contact at a female offenders home. She is on probation for an assault at a concert. She sees that you are hot and asks if you would like a glass of water to which you agree. Two minutes later she comes back with a cold glass of water which you rapidly drink. Within minutes you feel tired, woozy and if you are dissociating from your body. You think you may have been drugged.

What do you do?

Elements of Force:

Ability - an attacker possesses the power to injure or kill. This power may come in the form of a weapon (gun, knife, club, etc.) or through disparity of force.
- Does the subject have <u>ability</u> to do harm to you as the officer or to a third party?

        _____ Yes   _____ No

Opportunity - an attacker is capable of immediately employing the power to injure or kill. Two components to opportunity are distance and obstacles.
- Does the subject have <u>opportunity</u> to do harm to you as the officer or to a third party?

        _____ Yes   _____ No

Jeopardy - an attacker is acting in such a manner that a reasonable and prudent person would conclude he/she intends to injure or kill.
- Are you or a third party in jeopardy? _____ Yes   _____ No

Preclusion - officer assessment to determine if a lower level of force would be appropriate or ineffective; and retreat is not possible.

        What level of force is appropriate?

Scott Kirshner

- ♦ Is retreat possible?   ____ Yes   ____ No

Based on the scenario and the elements of force, what level of force on the use of force continuum is reasonable and necessary?

- _ Presence
- _ Verbal
- _ Empty Hand / Personal Weapons
- _ OC Spray
- _ Impact Weapon / Weapon of Opportunity
- _ Lethal Force

Notes: _____

_____

_____

_____

_____

_____

_____

_____

_____

_____

_____

_____

_____

_____

_____

_____

_____

_____

_____

134

Scenario #59: Cheap Shot

You have just taken a parolee into custody. He is handcuffed and a search for weapons has been completed. You are with one other parole officer. As you are escorting the offender to the transport vehicle he quickly turns around and kicks you in the groin.

What do you do?

Elements of Force:

Ability - an attacker possesses the power to injure or kill. This power may come in the form of a weapon (gun, knife, club, etc.) or through disparity of force.

- Does the subject have <u>ability</u> to do harm to you as the officer or to a third party?

    ____ Yes   ____ No

Opportunity - an attacker is capable of immediately employing the power to injure or kill. Two components to opportunity are distance and obstacles.

- Does the subject have <u>opportunity</u> to do harm to you as the officer or to a third party?

    ____ Yes   ____ No

Jeopardy - an attacker is acting in such a manner that a reasonable and prudent person would conclude he/she intends to injure or kill.

- Are you or a third party in jeopardy? ____ Yes   ____ No

Preclusion - officer assessment to determine if a lower level of force would be appropriate or ineffective; and retreat is not possible.

  What level of force is appropriate?

- Is retreat possible?   ____ Yes   ____ No

Based on the scenario and the elements of force, what level of force on the use of force continuum is reasonable and necessary?

_ Presence

_ Verbal

_ Empty Hand / Personal Weapons

_ OC Spray

_ Impact Weapon / Weapon of Opportunity

_ Lethal Force

Notes: _____

_____

_____

_____

_____

_____

_____

_____

_____

_____

_____

_____

_____

_____

_____

_____

_____

_____

_____

Scenario #60: Parolee with a Gun

You and another parole officer are conducting an unscheduled home contact on a parolee. When you get to the house the parolee lets you both in. Once you are both inside the residence and the door is shut the parole pulls out a handgun and is in the process of raising the weapon at you.

What do you do?

Elements of Force:

Ability - an attacker possesses the power to injure or kill. This power may come in the form of a weapon (gun, knife, club, etc.) or through disparity of force.

- ◆ Does the subject have <u>ability</u> to do harm to you as the officer or to a third party?

    ＿＿＿＿ Yes   ＿＿＿＿ No

Opportunity - an attacker is capable of immediately employing the power to injure or kill. Two components to opportunity are distance and obstacles.

- ◆ Does the subject have <u>opportunity</u> to do harm to you as the officer or to a third party?

    ＿＿＿＿ Yes   ＿＿＿＿ No

Jeopardy - an attacker is acting in such a manner that a reasonable and prudent person would conclude he/she intends to injure or kill.

- ◆ Are you or a third party in jeopardy? ＿＿＿＿ Yes   ＿＿＿＿ No

Preclusion - officer assessment to determine if a lower level of force would be appropriate or ineffective; and retreat is not possible.

What level of force is appropriate?

- ◆ Is retreat possible?   ＿＿＿＿ Yes   ＿＿＿＿ No

Based on the scenario and the elements of force, what level of force on the use of force continuum is reasonable and necessary?

_ Presence

_ Verbal

_ Empty Hand / Personal Weapons

_ OC Spray

_ Impact Weapon / Weapon of Opportunity

_ Lethal Force

Notes: _____

_____

_____

_____

_____

_____

_____

_____

_____

_____

_____

_____

_____

_____

_____

_____

_____

_____

Scenario #61: Office Arrest Shooter

You telephonically called a probationer into the office to conduct an office arrest. The probationer does not know that he is going to be taken into custody. You have five other probation officers that are going to assist with the arrest. The probationer reports to the office as directed and you escort him back to your office to conduct the arrest. Once in the office the probationer pulls out a firearm and starts shooting.

What do you do?

Elements of Force:

Ability - an attacker possesses the power to injure or kill. This power may come in the form of a weapon (gun, knife, club, etc.) or through disparity of force.

- ♦ Does the subject have <u>ability</u> to do harm to you as the officer or to a third party?

    _____ Yes   _____ No

Opportunity - an attacker is capable of immediately employing the power to injure or kill. Two components to opportunity are distance and obstacles.

- ♦ Does the subject have <u>opportunity</u> to do harm to you as the officer or to a third party?

    _____ Yes   _____ No

Jeopardy - an attacker is acting in such a manner that a reasonable and prudent person would conclude he/she intends to injure or kill.

- ♦ Are you or a third party in jeopardy? _____ Yes   _____ No

Preclusion - officer assessment to determine if a lower level of force would be appropriate or ineffective; and retreat is not possible.

    What level of force is appropriate?

- ♦ Is retreat possible?   _____ Yes   _____ No

Based on the scenario and the elements of force, what level of force on the use of force continuum is reasonable and necessary?

   _ Presence

   _ Verbal

   _ Empty Hand / Personal Weapons

   _ OC Spray

   _ Impact Weapon / Weapon of Opportunity

   _ Lethal Force

Notes: _____

_____

_____

_____

_____

_____

_____

_____

_____

_____

_____

_____

_____

_____

_____

_____

_____

Scenario #62: GUN, GUN

You and another parole officer go to a home of a parolee in order to arrest him for violating parole. Once inside the residence you inform the parolee that he is under arrest. Instead of complying he runs to his bedroom where you both chase him. As you enter the room you see a handgun on the bed. You yell, "GUN, GUN" to alert your partner.

What do you do?

Elements of Force:

Ability - an attacker possesses the power to injure or kill. This power may come in the form of a weapon (gun, knife, club, etc.) or through disparity of force.

- ♦ Does the subject have <u>ability</u> to do harm to you as the officer or to a third party?

    _____ Yes   _____ No

Opportunity - an attacker is capable of immediately employing the power to injure or kill. Two components to opportunity are distance and obstacles.

- ♦ Does the subject have <u>opportunity</u> to do harm to you as the officer or to a third party?

    _____ Yes   _____ No

Jeopardy - an attacker is acting in such a manner that a reasonable and prudent person would conclude he/she intends to injure or kill.

- ♦ Are you or a third party in jeopardy? _____ Yes   _____ No

Preclusion - officer assessment to determine if a lower level of force would be appropriate or ineffective; and retreat is not possible.

What level of force is appropriate?

- ♦ Is retreat possible?   _____ Yes   _____ No

Scott Kirshner

Based on the scenario and the elements cf force, what level of force on the use of force continuum is reasonable and necessary?

_ Presence

_ Verbal

_ Empty Hand / Personal Weapons

_ OC Spray

_ Impact Weapon / Weapon of Opportunity

_ Lethal Force

Notes: _____

_____

_____

_____

_____

_____

_____

_____

_____

_____

_____

_____

_____

_____

_____

_____

_____

_____

_____

Officer Survival Training Scenarios

<u>Scenario #63: Drug Paraphernalia</u>

You are alone conducting a home contact of a male who is on probation for possession of methamphetamine. Inside the house you are verifying his counseling, employment, and progress on probation. As you are preparing to leave you notice a syringe and a small baggie with powdery substance inside. The probationer notices that you saw the drug paraphernalia and he now appears to be very nervous.

What do you do?

Elements of Force:

Ability - an attacker possesses the power to injure or kill. This power may come in the form of a weapon (gun, knife, club, etc.) or through disparity of force.

- Does the subject have <u>ability</u> to do harm to you as the officer or to a third party?

  ____ Yes   ____ No

Opportunity - an attacker is capable of immediately employing the power to injure or kill. Two components to opportunity are distance and obstacles.

- Does the subject have <u>opportunity</u> to do harm to you as the officer or to a third party?

  ____ Yes   ____ No

Jeopardy - an attacker is acting in such a manner that a reasonable and prudent person would conclude he/she intends to injure or kill.

- Are you or a third party in jeopardy? ____ Yes   ____ No

Preclusion - officer assessment to determine if a lower level of force would be appropriate or ineffective; and retreat is not possible.

What level of force is appropriate?

- Is retreat possible?   ____ Yes   ____ No

Based on the scenario and the elements of force, what level of force on the use of force continuum is reasonable and necessary?

   _ Presence

   _ Verbal

   _ Empty Hand / Personal Weapons

   _ OC Spray

   _ Impact Weapon / Weapon of Opportunity

   _ Lethal Force

Notes: _____

_____

_____

_____

_____

_____

_____

_____

_____

_____

_____

_____

_____

_____

_____

_____

_____

Scenario #64: Borderline Personality Disorder

You are conducting a meeting with a 15 year old female juvenile who is on probation. Also in attendance is your supervisor, the juveniles mother and father, the school principle and a psychologist. The juvenile is on probation for assaulting a teacher, possession of drug paraphernalia, and possession of marijuana. She is diagnosed with Borderline Personality Disorder. While on probation she is being non-compliant with school, treatment, curfew, and she does not listen to her parents. For most of the meeting the juvenile was silent and just sitting in her chair staring at the desk. She did not make eye contact and refused to respond to questions. Out of nowhere she explosively jumps out of her seat and begins screaming, cursing and flailing her arms.

What do you do?

Elements of Force:

Ability - an attacker possesses the power to injure or kill. This power may come in the form of a weapon (gun, knife, club, etc.) or through disparity of force.

- ◆ Does the subject have ability to do harm to you as the officer or to a third party?

    _____ Yes   _____ No

Opportunity - an attacker is capable of immediately employing the power to injure or kill. Two components to opportunity are distance and obstacles.

- ◆ Does the subject have opportunity to do harm to you as the officer or to a third party?

    _____ Yes   _____ No

Jeopardy - an attacker is acting in such a manner that a reasonable and prudent person would conclude he/she intends to injure or kill.

- ◆ Are you or a third party in jeopardy? _____ Yes   _____ No

Preclusion - officer assessment to determine if a lower level of force would be appropriate or ineffective; and retreat is not possible.

Scott Kirshner

What level of force is appropriate?

♦   Is retreat possible?   ____ Yes   ____ No

Based on the scenario and the elements of force, what level of force on the use of force continuum is reasonable and necessary?

_ Presence

_ Verbal

_ Empty Hand / Personal Weapons

_ OC Spray

_ Impact Weapon / Weapon of Opportunity

_ Lethal Force

Notes: _____

_____

_____

_____

_____

_____

_____

_____

_____

_____

_____

_____

_____

_____

_____

_____

Scenario #65: Aryan Brotherhood

You are conducting a parolee contact at a halfway house on a member of the Aryan Brotherhood. You are with two other parole officers for additional safety. As you approach the parolee he stands up in an aggressive manner and demands you to come back another time. He then states, *"If you know what is best for all three of you then you will leave immediately. This isn't a game. Now go before all of you get hurt."* From his body language and tone you sense that the parolee is completely serious and that something is going on. You notice a baseball bat by the chair he was sitting.

What do you do?

Elements of Force:

Ability - an attacker possesses the power to injure or kill. This power may come in the form of a weapon (gun, knife, club, etc.) or through disparity of force.

   ♦   Does the subject have <u>ability</u> to do harm to you as the officer or to a third party?

   _____ Yes   _____ No

Opportunity - an attacker is capable of immediately employing the power to injure or kill. Two components to opportunity are distance and obstacles.

   ♦   Does the subject have <u>opportunity</u> to do harm to you as the officer or to a third party?

   _____ Yes   _____ No

Jeopardy - an attacker is acting in such a manner that a reasonable and prudent person would conclude he/she intends to injure or kill.

   ♦   Are you or a third party in jeopardy? _____ Yes   _____ No

Preclusion - officer assessment to determine if a lower level of force would be appropriate or ineffective; and retreat is not possible.

   What level of force is appropriate?

   ♦   Is retreat possible?   _____ Yes   _____ No

Scott Kirshner

Based on the scenario and the elements of force, what level of force on the use of force continuum is reasonable and necessary?

_ Presence

_ Verbal

_ Empty Hand / Personal Weapons

_ OC Spray

_ Impact Weapon / Weapon of Opportunity

_ Lethal Force

Notes: _____

_____

_____

_____

_____

_____

_____

_____

_____

_____

_____

_____

_____

_____

_____

_____

_____

_____

Scenario #66: Apartment Complex Shooting

You and another parole officer are conducting fieldwork together. You park your government vehicle at an apartment complex that houses offenders who are on both of your caseloads. As you are walking to make your first contact you see a male chasing another male who is running across the second floor walkway. They both run into a room and you hear three rapid fire gunshots.

What do you do?

Elements of Force:

Ability - an attacker possesses the power to injure or kill. This power may come in the form of a weapon (gun, knife, club, etc.) or through disparity of force.

- ♦ Does the subject have <u>ability</u> to do harm to you as the officer or to a third party?

    _____ Yes   _____ No

Opportunity - an attacker is capable of immediately employing the power to injure or kill. Two components to opportunity are distance and obstacles.

- ♦ Does the subject have <u>opportunity</u> to do harm to you as the officer or to a third party?

    _____ Yes   _____ No

Jeopardy - an attacker is acting in such a manner that a reasonable and prudent person would conclude he/she intends to injure or kill.

- ♦ Are you or a third party in jeopardy? _____ Yes   _____ No

Preclusion - officer assessment to determine if a lower level of force would be appropriate or ineffective; and retreat is not possible.

    What level of force is appropriate?

- ♦ Is retreat possible?   _____ Yes   _____ No

Based on the scenario and the elements of force, what level of force on the use of force continuum is reasonable and necessary?

    _ Presence

    _ Verbal

    _ Empty Hand / Personal Weapons

    _ OC Spray

    _ Impact Weapon / Weapon of Opportunity

    _ Lethal Force

Notes: _____

_____

_____

_____

_____

_____

_____

_____

_____

_____

_____

_____

_____

_____

_____

_____

_____

_____

Scenario #67: "Yes, I'm Threatening You"

You and a probationer are in an interview room where you are issuing the offender a Probation Violation Warning for a positive drug test for marijuana and missing his last scheduled office contact. The offender tells you that, "*Writing me up is not a good idea and it is not in your best interest.*" You ask the offender why this is the case. The offender replies, "*Because I know exactly where you live on Parsons Blvd.*" You ask the offender if he is threatening you and he replies, "*Yes, I'm threatening you.*" During the contact the offender was very calm and relaxed but you know he was serious.

What do you do?

Elements of Force:

Ability - an attacker possesses the power to injure or kill. This power may come in the form of a weapon (gun, knife, club, etc.) or through disparity of force.

- Does the subject have <u>ability</u> to do harm to you as the officer or to a third party?

    ____ Yes   ____ No

Opportunity - an attacker is capable of immediately employing the power to injure or kill. Two components to opportunity are distance and obstacles.

- Does the subject have <u>opportunity</u> to do harm to you as the officer or to a third party?

    ____ Yes   ____ No

Jeopardy - an attacker is acting in such a manner that a reasonable and prudent person would conclude he/she intends to injure or kill.

- Are you or a third party in jeopardy? ____ Yes   ____ No

Preclusion - officer assessment to determine if a lower level of force would be appropriate or ineffective; and retreat is not possible.

    What level of force is appropriate?

- Is retreat possible?   ____ Yes   ____ No

Scott Kirshner

Based on the scenario and the elements of force, what level of force on the use of force continuum is reasonable and necessary?

_ Presence

_ Verbal

_ Empty Hand / Personal Weapons

_ OC Spray

_ Impact Weapon / Weapon of Opportunity

_ Lethal Force

Notes: _____

_____

_____

_____

_____

_____

_____

_____

_____

_____

_____

_____

_____

_____

_____

_____

_____

_____

_____

Scenario #68: No Where To Go

You are assigned to the departments Warrants Unit. On your way to a briefing with the local police department you notice an offender who has an active warrant driving a vehicle next to you. You contact the police officers that you are meeting by telephone and alert them of the situation. Your plan is to follow the vehicle until the police officers arrive in their unmarked police cars. You are stopped at a red light and the offenders vehicle is directly in front of you. There are cars all around your vehicle and you are boxed in. The offender puts his vehicle in reverse and repeatedly is backing into your vehicle. You cannot back up and both sides are blocked.

What do you do?

Elements of Force:

Ability - an attacker possesses the power to injure or kill. This power may come in the form of a weapon (gun, knife, club, etc.) or through disparity of force.

- Does the subject have <u>ability</u> to do harm to you as the officer or to a third party?

    ____ Yes   ____ No

Opportunity - an attacker is capable of immediately employing the power to injure or kill. Two components to opportunity are distance and obstacles.

- Does the subject have <u>opportunity</u> to do harm to you as the officer or to a third party?

    ____ Yes   ____ No

Jeopardy - an attacker is acting in such a manner that a reasonable and prudent person would conclude he/she intends to injure or kill.

- Are you or a third party in jeopardy? ____ Yes   ____ No

Preclusion - officer assessment to determine if a lower level of force would be appropriate or ineffective; and retreat is not possible.

  What level of force is appropriate?

♦ Is retreat possible? _____ Yes   _____ No

Based on the scenario and the elements of force, what level of force on the use of force continuum is reasonable and necessary?

_ Presence

_ Verbal

_ Empty Hand / Personal Weapons

_ OC Spray

_ Impact Weapon / Weapon of Opportunity

_ Lethal Force

Notes: _____

_____

_____

_____

_____

_____

_____

_____

_____

_____

_____

_____

_____

_____

_____

_____

_____

Scenario #69: OC Spray

You are conducting a home contact on a parolee at his apartment. The parolee is a body builder and is in excellent physical condition. During the contact the parolee begins arguing with you stating that you are always nitpicking and looking for problems. You see that he is getting upset so you attempt to leave. As you leave the apartment the offender is follow you and aggressively yells, "*Don't walk away from me when I'm talking to you.*" You feel that he is aggressive and becoming a danger. You spray him in the face with OC spray. The offender wipes his face, smiles and says, "*Fuck you, the fight is on.*" He then aggressively moves toward you.

What do you do?

Elements of Force:

Ability - an attacker possesses the power to injure or kill. This power may come in the form of a weapon (gun, knife, club, etc.) or through disparity of force.

- ◆ Does the subject have <u>ability</u> to do harm to you as the officer or to a third party?

    ____ Yes   ____ No

Opportunity - an attacker is capable of immediately employing the power to injure or kill. Two components to opportunity are distance and obstacles.

- ◆ Does the subject have <u>opportunity</u> to do harm to you as the officer or to a third party?

    ____ Yes   ____ No

Jeopardy - an attacker is acting in such a manner that a reasonable and prudent person would conclude he/she intends to injure or kill.

- ◆ Are you or a third party in jeopardy? ____ Yes   ____ No

Preclusion - officer assessment to determine if a lower level of force would be appropriate or ineffective; and retreat is not possible.

    What level of force is appropriate?

♦ Is retreat possible? _____ Yes _____ No .

Based on the scenario and the elements of force, what level of force on the use of force continuum is reasonable and necessary?

_ Presence

_ Verbal

_ Empty Hand / Personal Weapons

_ OC Spray

_ Impact Weapon / Weapon of Opportunity

_ Lethal Force

Notes: _____

_____

_____

_____

_____

_____

_____

_____

_____

_____

_____

_____

_____

_____

_____

_____

_____

_____

_____

Scenario #70: Frustrated

You are conducting an initial contact with a newly assigned offender. During this contact you explain all the rules and requirements of probation. This is a standard contact that you have done hundreds if not thousands of times. You give the offender a directive to attend substance abuse counseling based on his charge of an Aggravated DUI and the assessment that was conducted. The offender is adamant that he does not need treatment and that he does not have a problem with alcohol. He begins to yell at you stating, *"I don't need treatment. You are just a PO. You're not an expert. You don't know what you are doing and I don't need treatment. I'm not going."* The offenders face is beat red and he looks very frustrated.

What do you do?

Elements of Force:

Ability - an attacker possesses the power to injure or kill. This power may come in the form of a weapon (gun, knife, club, etc.) or through disparity of force.

- ♦ Does the subject have <u>ability</u> to do harm to you as the officer or to a third party?

    _____ Yes   _____ No

Opportunity - an attacker is capable of immediately employing the power to injure or kill. Two components to opportunity are distance and obstacles.

- ♦ Does the subject have <u>opportunity</u> to do harm to you as the officer or to a third party?

    _____ Yes   _____ No

Jeopardy - an attacker is acting in such a manner that a reasonable and prudent person would conclude he/she intends to injure or kill.

- ♦ Are you or a third party in jeopardy? _____ Yes   _____ No

Preclusion - officer assessment to determine if a lower level of force would be appropriate or ineffective; and retreat is not possible.

What level of force is appropriate?

♦ Is retreat possible? _____ Yes _____ No

Based on the scenario and the elements of force, what level of force on the use of force continuum is reasonable and necessary?

_ Presence

_ Verbal

_ Empty Hand / Personal Weapons

_ OC Spray

_ Impact Weapon / Weapon of Opportunity

_ Lethal Force

Notes: _____

_____

_____

_____

_____

_____

_____

_____

_____

_____

_____

_____

_____

_____

_____

_____

Scenario #71: Handshake

You are having a first contact with a new parolee just released from prison after serving a 15 year sentence. You call the offender from the lobby and escort him to your office. When you introduce yourself he extends his hand for a handshake. You reciprocate and shake his hand. The parole has an iron grip on your hand and stares at you for approximately 5 seconds when he says to you, *"Behave appropriately or there will be problems."*

What do you do?

Elements of Force:

Ability - an attacker possesses the power to injure or kill. This power may come in the form of a weapon (gun, knife, club, etc.) or through disparity of force.

♦   Does the subject have ability to do harm to you as the officer or to a third party?

_____ Yes   _____ No

Opportunity - an attacker is capable of immediately employing the power to injure or kill. Two components to opportunity are distance and obstacles.

♦   Does the subject have opportunity to do harm to you as the officer or to a third party?

_____ Yes   _____ No

Jeopardy - an attacker is acting in such a manner that a reasonable and prudent person would conclude he/she intends to injure or kill.

♦   Are you or a third party in jeopardy? _____ Yes   _____ No

Preclusion - officer assessment to determine if a lower level of force would be appropriate or ineffective; and retreat is not possible.

What level of force is appropriate?

♦   Is retreat possible?   _____ Yes   _____ No

Based on the scenario and the elements of force, what level of force on the use of force continuum is reasonable and necessary?

     _ Presence

     _ Verbal

     _ Empty Hand / Personal Weapons

     _ OC Spray

     _ Impact Weapon / Weapon of Opportunity

     _ Lethal Force

Notes: _____

_____

_____

_____

_____

_____

_____

_____

_____

_____

_____

_____

_____

_____

_____

_____

_____

Scenario #72: Multiple Attackers

You just concluded a contact with a probationer at his apartment. The apartment is located in a high crime area known for drugs, gangs, and violence. As you are walking back to your vehicle you are suddenly attacked by 5 men.

What do you do?

Elements of Force:

Ability - an attacker possesses the power to injure or kill. This power may come in the form of a weapon (gun, knife, club, etc.) or through disparity of force.

- ◆ Does the subject have <u>ability</u> to do harm to you as the officer or to a third party?

    ____ Yes   ____ No

Opportunity - an attacker is capable of immediately employing the power to injure or kill. Two components to opportunity are distance and obstacles.

- ◆ Does the subject have <u>opportunity</u> to do harm to you as the officer or to a third party?

    ____ Yes   ____ No

Jeopardy - an attacker is acting in such a manner that a reasonable and prudent person would conclude he/she intends to injure or kill.

- ◆ Are you or a third party in jeopardy? ____ Yes   ____ No

Preclusion - officer assessment to determine if a lower level of force would be appropriate or ineffective; and retreat is not possible.

    What level of force is appropriate?

- ◆ Is retreat possible?   ____ Yes   ____ No

Based on the scenario and the elements of force, what level of force on the use of force continuum is reasonable and necessary?

_ Presence

_ Verbal

_ Empty Hand / Personal Weapons

_ OC Spray

_ Impact Weapon / Weapon of Opportunity

_ Lethal Force

Notes: _____

_____

_____

_____

_____

_____

_____

_____

_____

_____

_____

_____

_____

_____

_____

_____

_____

_____

Scenario #73: Sucker Punch

You supervise a very rural and remote caseload. You are conducting a residential contact on a juvenile who has been very compliant while on probation. To get to the house you have to drive 5 miles on a remote dirt road. You pull up to the house and exit your vehicle. A male comes out of nowhere and punches you in the face. You are dizzy from the punch.

What do you do?

<u>Elements of Force:</u>

Ability - an attacker possesses the power to injure or kill. This power may come in the form of a weapon (gun, knife, club, etc.) or through disparity of force.

♦ Does the subject have <u>ability</u> to do harm to you as the officer or to a third party?

_____ Yes _____ No

Opportunity - an attacker is capable of immediately employing the power to injure or kill. Two components to opportunity are distance and obstacles.

♦ Does the subject have <u>opportunity</u> to do harm to you as the officer or to a third party?

_____ Yes _____ No

Jeopardy - an attacker is acting in such a manner that a reasonable and prudent person would conclude he/she intends to injure or kill.

♦ Are you or a third party in jeopardy? _____ Yes _____ No

Preclusion - officer assessment to determine if a lower level of force would be appropriate or ineffective; and retreat is not possible.

What level of force is appropriate?

♦ Is retreat possible? _____ Yes _____ No

Based on the scenario and the elements of force, what level of force on the use of force continuum is reasonable and necessary?

     _ Presence

     _ Verbal

     _ Empty Hand / Personal Weapons

     _ OC Spray

     _ Impact Weapon / Weapon of Opportunity

     _ Lethal Force

Notes: _____

_____

_____

_____

_____

_____

_____

_____

_____

_____

_____

_____

_____

_____

_____

_____

_____

_____

_____

_____

Scenario #74: Light Distraction

It is 1:00PM on a bright sunny day. You knock on the front door of an offenders residence who is on probation for manufacturing methamphetamine. The door opens and it is dark inside especially since your eyes have not had time to adjust. All of a sudden a bright light is blasted in your eyes and you feel someone grab you and pull you into the residence.

What do you do?

Elements of Force:

Ability - an attacker possesses the power to injure or kill. This power may come in the form of a weapon (gun, knife, club, etc.) or through disparity of force.

- ♦ Does the subject have <u>ability</u> to do harm to you as the officer or to a third party?

    ____ Yes   ____ No

Opportunity - an attacker is capable of immediately employing the power to injure or kill. Two components to opportunity are distance and obstacles.

- ♦ Does the subject have <u>opportunity</u> to do harm to you as the officer or to a third party?

    ____ Yes   ____ No

Jeopardy - an attacker is acting in such a manner that a reasonable and prudent person would conclude he/she intends to injure or kill.

- ♦ Are you or a third party in jeopardy? ____ Yes   ____ No

Preclusion - officer assessment to determine if a lower level of force would be appropriate or ineffective; and retreat is not possible.

    What level of force is appropriate?

- ♦ Is retreat possible?   ____ Yes   ____ No

Based on the scenario and the elements of force, what level of force on the use of force continuum is reasonable and necessary?

      _ Presence

      _ Verbal

      _ Empty Hand / Personal Weapons

      _ OC Spray

      _ Impact Weapon / Weapon of Opportunity

      _ Lethal Force

Notes: _____

_____

_____

_____

_____

_____

_____

_____

_____

_____

_____

_____

_____

_____

_____

_____

_____

Scenario #75: Attempted Gun Grab

You are armed with a firearm and conducting a residential contact at the home of a parolee. In the home is the parolee, his wife and his two teenage kids. The parolee has been struggling with compliance and is close to having his parole revoked. During the contact you are both standing in the dining room. While you feel that the contact is going well and uneventful the parole suddenly attempts to grab your firearm. Your weapon is still in the holster but the parole has a solid grip on the weapon.

What do you do?

Elements of Force:

Ability - an attacker possesses the power to injure or kill. This power may come in the form of a weapon (gun, knife, club, etc.) or through disparity of force.

- ♦ Does the subject have <u>ability</u> to do harm to you as the officer or to a third party?

    _____ Yes   _____ No

Opportunity - an attacker is capable of immediately employing the power to injure or kill. Two components to opportunity are distance and obstacles.

- ♦ Does the subject have <u>opportunity</u> to do harm to you as the officer or to a third party?

    _____ Yes   _____ No

Jeopardy - an attacker is acting in such a manner that a reasonable and prudent person would conclude he/she intends to injure or kill.

- ♦ Are you or a third party in jeopardy? _____ Yes   _____ No

Preclusion - officer assessment to determine if a lower level of force would be appropriate or ineffective; and retreat is not possible.

    What level of force is appropriate?

- ♦ Is retreat possible?   _____ Yes   _____ No

Based on the scenario and the elements of force, what level of force on the use of force continuum is reasonable and necessary?

    _ Presence

    _ Verbal

    _ Empty Hand / Personal Weapons

    _ OC Spray

    _ Impact Weapon / Weapon of Opportunity

    _ Lethal Force

Notes: _____

_____

_____

_____

_____

_____

_____

_____

_____

_____

_____

_____

_____

_____

_____

_____

_____

_____

Scenario #76: Stabbed

You are meeting with a probationer in your office and giving him a written directive to enter relapse prevention after receiving a positive drug test for methamphetamine and cocaine. The probationer recently complete a six month intensive outpatient treatment program with no positive drug tests. The offender says that he just partied with some friend and does not need relapse prevention. You insist that relapse prevention is required. The probationer angrily grabs a pen off your desk to sign the paperwork but instead uses the pen the stab you in the chest. The pen penetrated your chest which is now bleeding and you are in significant pain.

What do you do?

Elements of Force:

Ability - an attacker possesses the power to injure or kill. This power may come in the form of a weapon (gun, knife, club, etc.) or through disparity of force.

- ♦ Does the subject have ability to do harm to you as the officer or to a third party?

    _____ Yes   _____ No

Opportunity - an attacker is capable of immediately employing the power to injure or kill. Two components to opportunity are distance and obstacles.

- ♦ Does the subject have opportunity to do harm to you as the officer or to a third party?

    _____ Yes   _____ No

Jeopardy - an attacker is acting in such a manner that a reasonable and prudent person would conclude he/she intends to injure or kill.

- ♦ Are you or a third party in jeopardy? _____ Yes   _____ No

Preclusion - officer assessment to determine if a lower level of force would be appropriate or ineffective; and retreat is not possible.

    What level of force is appropriate?

- ♦ Is retreat possible? _____ Yes _____ No

Based on the scenario and the elements of force, what level of force on the use of force continuum is reasonable and necessary?

_ Presence

_ Verbal

_ Empty Hand / Personal Weapons

_ OC Spray

_ Impact Weapon / Weapon of Opportunity

_ Lethal Force

Notes: _____

_____

_____

_____

_____

_____

_____

_____

_____

_____

_____

_____

_____

_____

_____

_____

_____

Scenario #77: Pregnant Juvenile

You are conducting an office contact with a 16 year old juvenile who is seven months pregnant. Since day one on probation the juvenile has been defiant. She does not get along with her parents and refuses to attend school so that she can graduate. As you are discussing the importance of an education the juvenile attacks you by scratching your face and pulling your hair. When she scratched your face she poked you in the eye and your vision is blurry.

What do you do?

Elements of Force:

Ability - an attacker possesses the power to injure or kill. This power may come in the form of a weapon (gun, knife, club, etc.) or through disparity of force.

- ♦ Does the subject have <u>ability</u> to do harm to you as the officer or to a third party?

    _____ Yes   _____ No

Opportunity - an attacker is capable of immediately employing the power to injure or kill. Two components to opportunity are distance and obstacles.

- ♦ Does the subject have <u>opportunity</u> to do harm to you as the officer or to a third party?

    _____ Yes   _____ No

Jeopardy - an attacker is acting in such a manner that a reasonable and prudent person would conclude he/she intends to injure or kill.

- ♦ Are you or a third party in jeopardy? _____ Yes   _____ No

Preclusion - officer assessment to determine if a lower level of force would be appropriate or ineffective; and retreat is not possible.

    What level of force is appropriate?

- ♦ Is retreat possible?   _____ Yes   _____ No

Based on the scenario and the elements of force, what level of force on the use of force continuum is reasonable and necessary?

_ Presence

_ Verbal

_ Empty Hand / Personal Weapons

_ OC Spray

_ Impact Weapon / Weapon of Opportunity

_ Lethal Force

Notes: _____

_____

_____

_____

_____

_____

_____

_____

_____

_____

_____

_____

_____

_____

_____

_____

_____

_____

Scenario #78: Do You Have a Light?

You just concluded a meeting with an employer who regularly hires felons. This employer has been a valuable resource in hiring offenders with criminal records and you have a very positive relationship. After the meeting you are walking back to your vehicle when a male in his 30's asks you for a light. As you are about to tell him that you do not smoke you are hit from behind in the head with a hammer.

What do you do?

Elements of Force:

Ability - an attacker possesses the power to injure or kill. This power may come in the form of a weapon (gun, knife, club, etc.) or through disparity of force.

- Does the subject have <u>ability</u> to do harm to you as the officer or to a third party?

    ____ Yes   ____ No

Opportunity - an attacker is capable of immediately employing the power to injure or kill. Two components to opportunity are distance and obstacles.

- Does the subject have <u>opportunity</u> to do harm to you as the officer or to a third party?

    ____ Yes   ____ No

Jeopardy - an attacker is acting in such a manner that a reasonable and prudent person would conclude he/she intends to injure or kill.

- Are you or a third party in jeopardy? ____ Yes   ____ No

Preclusion - officer assessment to determine if a lower level of force would be appropriate or ineffective; and retreat is not possible.

    What level of force is appropriate?

- Is retreat possible?   ____ Yes   ____ No

Based on the scenario and the elements of force, what level of force on the use of force continuum is reasonable and necessary?

  _ Presence

  _ Verbal

  _ Empty Hand / Personal Weapons

  _ OC Spray

  _ Impact Weapon / Weapon of Opportunity

  _ Lethal Force

Notes: _____

_____

_____

_____

_____

_____

_____

_____

_____

_____

_____

_____

_____

_____

_____

_____

_____

_____

_____

Scenario #79: Fight at Group Class

You are observing a substance abuse treatment group class in which two offenders assigned to your caseload are attending. During the class two participants get into a verbal altercation. The therapist is not able to get the participants under control and a physical fight breaks out but it does not consist of the offenders on your caseload.

What do you do?

Elements of Force:

Ability - an attacker possesses the power to injure or kill. This power may come in the form of a weapon (gun, knife, club, etc.) or through disparity of force.

♦ Does the subject have <u>ability</u> to do harm to you as the officer or to a third party?

_____ Yes   _____ No

Opportunity - an attacker is capable of immediately employing the power to injure or kill. Two components to opportunity are distance and obstacles.

♦ Does the subject have <u>opportunity</u> to do harm to you as the officer or to a third party?

_____ Yes   _____ No

Jeopardy - an attacker is acting in such a manner that a reasonable and prudent person would conclude he/she intends to injure or kill.

♦ Are you or a third party in jeopardy? _____ Yes   _____ No

Preclusion - officer assessment to determine if a lower level of force would be appropriate or ineffective; and retreat is not possible.

What level of force is appropriate?

♦ Is retreat possible?   _____ Yes   _____ No

Based on the scenario and the elements of force, what level of force on the use of force continuum is reasonable and necessary?

    _ Presence

    _ Verbal

    _ Empty Hand / Personal Weapons

    _ OC Spray

    _ Impact Weapon / Weapon of Opportunity

    _ Lethal Force

Notes: _____

_____

_____

_____

_____

_____

_____

_____

_____

_____

_____

_____

_____

_____

_____

_____

_____

_____

Scenario #80: Angry Tirade

You are conducting office day and have a female offender in your office. The offender has two unexcused absences for failing to attend treatment classes. Her counselor has called you to let you know and to state that the offender will be dropped from treatment if she has one more unexcused absence. As you are discussing this with the offender she begins to scream at you stating that her car is broken and she can't get to counseling because it is 10 miles from her house. You try to verbally de-escalate the offender but it is not working.

What do you do?

Elements of Force:

Ability - an attacker possesses the power to injure or kill. This power may come in the form of a weapon (gun, knife, club, etc.) or through disparity of force.

♦ Does the subject have <u>ability</u> to do harm to you as the officer or to a third party?

____ Yes   ____ No

Opportunity - an attacker is capable of immediately employing the power to injure or kill. Two components to opportunity are distance and obstacles.

♦ Does the subject have <u>opportunity</u> to do harm to you as the officer or to a third party?

____ Yes   ____ No

Jeopardy - an attacker is acting in such a manner that a reasonable and prudent person would conclude he/she intends to injure or kill.

♦ Are you or a third party in jeopardy? ____ Yes   ____ No

Preclusion - officer assessment to determine if a lower level of force would be appropriate or ineffective; and retreat is not possible.

What level of force is appropriate?

♦ Is retreat possible?   ____ Yes   ____ No

Based on the scenario and the elements of force, what level of force on the use of force continuum is reasonable and necessary?

　_ Presence

　_ Verbal

　_ Empty Hand / Personal Weapons

　_ OC Spray

　_ Impact Weapon / Weapon of Opportunity

　_ Lethal Force

Notes: _____

_____

_____

_____

_____

_____

_____

_____

_____

_____

_____

_____

_____

_____

_____

_____

_____

_____

_____

Scenario #81: Shot

You are conducting a field contact at an apartment complex. The offender that you are contacting has been on your caseload for 8 months and has been compliant. You are conducting an address verification as the offender has recently moved into the apartment complex. As you knock on the front door a bullet is shot from inside of the apartment striking you in the leg. The front door was never opened and you are severely bleeding but still able to move.

What do you do?

Elements of Force:

Ability - an attacker possesses the power to injure or kill. This power may come in the form of a weapon (gun, knife, club, etc.) or through disparity of force.

- Does the subject have <u>ability</u> to do harm to you as the officer or to a third party?

    ____ Yes   ____ No

Opportunity - an attacker is capable of immediately employing the power to injure or kill. Two components to opportunity are distance and obstacles.

- Does the subject have <u>opportunity</u> to do harm to you as the officer or to a third party?

    ____ Yes   ____ No

Jeopardy - an attacker is acting in such a manner that a reasonable and prudent person would conclude he/she intends to injure or kill.

- Are you or a third party in jeopardy? ____ Yes   ____ No

Preclusion - officer assessment to determine if a lower level of force would be appropriate or ineffective; and retreat is not possible.

What level of force is appropriate?

- Is retreat possible?   ____ Yes   ____ No

Based on the scenario and the elements of force, what level of force on the use of force continuum is reasonable and necessary?

      _ Presence

      _ Verbal

      _ Empty Hand / Personal Weapons

      _ OC Spray

      _ Impact Weapon / Weapon of Opportunity

      _ Lethal Force

Notes: _____

_____

_____

_____

_____

_____

_____

_____

_____

_____

_____

_____

_____

_____

_____

_____

_____

Scenario #82: Residential Search – Secret Room

You are part of a search team that is searching a 2,500 residential home in an upper middle class neighborhood. The home has a security system which includes video cameras. During the search you notice a covert video camera in the corner of a closet. As you search the closet you notice a hidden door. You and another officer open the door which leads to a staircase that goes to a lower level. As you walk down the stairs you notice a naked female chained to a bed and gagged so that she cannot speak.

What do you do?

Elements of Force:

Ability - an attacker possesses the power to injure or kill. This power may come in the form of a weapon (gun, knife, club, etc.) or through disparity of force.

♦ Does the subject have <u>ability</u> to do harm to you as the officer or to a third party?

_____ Yes   _____ No

Opportunity - an attacker is capable of immediately employing the power to injure or kill. Two components to opportunity are distance and obstacles.

♦ Does the subject have <u>opportunity</u> to do harm to you as the officer or to a third party?

_____ Yes   _____ No

Jeopardy - an attacker is acting in such a manner that a reasonable and prudent person would conclude he/she intends to injure or kill.

♦ Are you or a third party in jeopardy? _____ Yes   _____ No

Preclusion - officer assessment to determine if a lower level of force would be appropriate or ineffective; and retreat is not possible.

What level of force is appropriate?

♦ Is retreat possible?   _____ Yes   _____ No

Based on the scenario and the elements of force, what level of force on the use of force continuum is reasonable and necessary?

_ Presence

_ Verbal

_ Empty Hand / Personal Weapons

_ OC Spray

_ Impact Weapon / Weapon of Opportunity

_ Lethal Force

Notes: _____

_____

_____

_____

_____

_____

_____

_____

_____

_____

_____

_____

_____

_____

_____

_____

_____

_____

Scenario #83: I Spy a Firearm

You are conducting a residential contact on a 15 year old female who is on probation for truancy. When you knock on the front door the juvenile's father answers the door. You have been at the residence numerous times. The juvenile has been mostly compliant and the parents have been very active and helpful. When the father opens the front door you notice a handgun on a stand next to the front door. The father does not notice that you saw the weapon.

What do you do?

Elements of Force:

Ability - an attacker possesses the power to injure or kill. This power may come in the form of a weapon (gun, knife, club, etc.) or through disparity of force.

♦ Does the subject have <u>ability</u> to do harm to you as the officer or to a third party?

_____ Yes   _____ No

Opportunity - an attacker is capable of immediately employing the power to injure or kill. Two components to opportunity are distance and obstacles.

♦ Does the subject have <u>opportunity</u> to do harm to you as the officer or to a third party?

_____ Yes   _____ No

Jeopardy - an attacker is acting in such a manner that a reasonable and prudent person would conclude he/she intends to injure or kill.

♦ Are you or a third party in jeopardy? _____ Yes   _____ No

Preclusion - officer assessment to determine if a lower level of force would be appropriate or ineffective; and retreat is not possible.

What level of force is appropriate?

♦ Is retreat possible?   _____ Yes   _____ No

Based on the scenario and the elements of force, what level of force on the use of force continuum is reasonable and necessary?

_ Presence

_ Verbal

_ Empty Hand / Personal Weapons

_ OC Spray

_ Impact Weapon / Weapon of Opportunity

_ Lethal Force

Notes: _____

_____

_____

_____

_____

_____

_____

_____

_____

_____

_____

_____

_____

_____

_____

_____

_____

Scenario #84: Drug Dealer

You are conducting a residential contact on an parolee with a long history of selling drugs. Before approaching the house you park down the street to watch the house for a few minutes using a pair of binoculars. Within 10 minutes you see three different vehicles come and go. Each time an individual goes to the front door and is let inside. Each time the person is in the house for less than one minute and then gets back in their vehicle to leave.

What do you do?

Elements of Force:

Ability - an attacker possesses the power to injure or kill. This power may come in the form of a weapon (gun, knife, club, etc.) or through disparity of force.

- ◆ Does the subject have <u>ability</u> to do harm to you as the officer or to a third party?

    _____ Yes   _____ No

Opportunity - an attacker is capable of immediately employing the power to injure or kill. Two components to opportunity are distance and obstacles.

- ◆ Does the subject have <u>opportunity</u> to do harm to you as the officer or to a third party?

    _____ Yes   _____ No

Jeopardy - an attacker is acting in such a manner that a reasonable and prudent person would conclude he/she intends to injure or kill.

- ◆ Are you or a third party in jeopardy? _____ Yes   _____ No

Preclusion - officer assessment to determine if a lower level of force would be appropriate or ineffective; and retreat is not possible.

    What level of force is appropriate?

- ◆ Is retreat possible?   _____ Yes   _____ No

Based on the scenario and the elements of force, what level of force on the use of force continuum is reasonable and necessary?

　　　_ Presence

　　　_ Verbal

　　　_ Empty Hand / Personal Weapons

　　　_ OC Spray

　　　_ Impact Weapon / Weapon of Opportunity

　　　_ Lethal Force

Notes: _____

_____

_____

_____

_____

_____

_____

_____

_____

_____

_____

_____

_____

_____

_____

_____

_____

_____

<u>Officer Safety Training Violations</u>

When attending department safety training or private law enforcement training classes the instructor is responsible for providing all of the participants the safety rules for the training. Safety of all the participants, instructors and role-players are paramount during training classes. This helps to minimize potential injury and distraction to officers who are attending. These safety instructions are extremely important and must be adhered to during the training. Yet, every year we hear stories of law enforcement officers killed or injured during officer safety training classes. Many times these events are preventable.

It is important to understand that safety is everyone's responsibility. If you see a safety violation you have a definitive obligation to speak up. But, some officers are not comfortable being assertive even when it means that someone's life may be saved. The following scenarios are designed to get you to talk about situations that you may encounter in a training environment that are not safe. This will help you successfully resolve such situations with the ultimate goal of keeping everyone in the training safe from potential injury or death.

Scenario #85: Safety Violation

You are an armed officer attending departmental force-on-force training. In this training you will be using Non-Lethal Training Ammunition such as SIMUNITION. During this training no weapons or ammunition of any kind are allowed in the training area. The Safety Officer is talking with another trainer as he is searching participants. You notice that he fails to see that another officer brought in his duty weapon which is not only a clear violation of the safety rules but it is an extreme safety violation.

What do you do?

Course of Action: _____

_____

_____

_____

_____

_____

_____

_____

_____

_____

_____

Scenario #86: Finger on Trigger

You are an armed officer attending departmental range training. At the beginning of class the Lead Firearms Instructor goes over all the safety rules of the class to ensure officer safety. During one of the drills an officer is required to shoot from behind cover, reload, move to another item of cover and engage a target. As you are watching an officer do this you notice that he ran from his location behind cover to another location of cover with his finger on the trigger.

What do you do?

Course of Action: _____

_____

_____

_____

_____

_____

_____

_____

_____

_____

_____

_____

_____

_____

_____

Scott Kirshner

Scenario #87: Defensive Tactics

You are attending a defensive tactics refresher class. You are teamed up with an officer who is known to have an ego and show off. During a particular drill the officer that you are teamed up with is hitting you way too hard during an exercise. You tell him to "*lighten up*" but on the next drill he hits you hard enough to knock the air out of your lungs.

What do you do?

Course of Action: _____

_____

_____

_____

_____

_____

_____

_____

_____

_____

_____

_____

_____

_____

_____

Scenario #88: Muzzle Discipline

You are attending a department firearms training class. The range safety officer has stressed that you are to point your muzzle in a safe direction at all times. During a drill you notice one particular officer who is covering other officers with his muzzle. As this officer is moving from target to target his muzzle was pointed at other officers despite the directions from the instructor.

What do you do?

Course of Action: _____

_____

_____

_____

_____

_____

_____

_____

_____

_____

_____

_____

_____

_____

_____

_____

_____

<u>Scenario #89: Edged Weapons Defense</u>

You are attending a department training class specifically for defending against edged weapons. The instructor states that the only drills that are to be practiced in class are the ones that are taught in class. You are teamed up with an officer who has taken martial arts for many years. This officer is constantly trying to show you "better and more effective" ways to protect yourself from an edged weapons attack. The information is completely different from what is being taught.

What do you do?

Course of Action: _____

_____

_____

_____

_____

_____

_____

_____

_____

_____

_____

_____

_____

_____

_____

Scenario #90: Your Dead...Again

During a scenario based training class you are in a situation where an offender stabs you with a knife before you could access your firearm. Immediately after the scenario another officer yells at you, "*Your dead...again*!" This officer has been making such comments throughout the training but no one has said anything to either the officer or the trainers. And, no trainer has said anything to the officer regarding his negative comments. But, the rest of the officers are not happy with these comments.

What do you do?

Course of Action: _____

_____

_____

_____

_____

_____

_____

_____

_____

_____

_____

_____

_____

_____

Scenario #91: Takedown

During a training class you are initiating an arrest on a noncompliant subject. In the process you perform a takedown which causes the roleplayer to hit his head just off the edge of the training mat. You see the roleplayers eyes roll back and he appears injured.

What do you do?

Course of Action: _____

_____

_____

_____

_____

_____

_____

_____

_____

_____

_____

_____

_____

_____

_____

_____

Scenario #92: Incorrect Technique

You are attending an annual defensive tactics refresher training. The instructor is reviewing a handcuffing technique that you know is incorrect and not safe. The way it is being presented places the officer in a potentially dangerous situation.

What do you do?

Course of Action: _____

_____

_____

_____

_____

_____

_____

_____

_____

_____

_____

_____

_____

_____

_____

_____

_____

_____

_____

Scenario #93: Weapons Malfunction

During a firearms training class you are on a static range performing a drill where you fire two rounds into the body and then one round to the head. The officer on the left of you has a jam and cannot clear his weapon. He turns to you to ask for assistance and in the process his weapon is pointed at your chest.

What do you do?

Course of Action: _____

_____

_____

_____

_____

_____

_____

_____

_____

_____

_____

_____

_____

_____

_____

_____

_____

Scenario #94: Failing to Perform

You are part of your departments Fugitive Apprehension Unit. You are a tight group that often trains together. During a training where you are practicing building searches and clearing a member of the unit is failing to perform up to standards. This officer is older and has not been performing well for a while. Everyone on the team likes this officer a lot but he is now an obvious safety risk.

What do you do?

Course of Action: _____

_____

_____

_____

_____

_____

_____

_____

_____

_____

_____

_____

_____

_____

_____

Scenario #95: Weapon Disarming

You are attending a department training class that focuses on weapon disarming. Protocol and policy states that only "Red Guns" will be used in this training and that officers are not authorized to bring in real firearms or any ammunition. During the class you and your partner do not have a Red Gun because there are not enough to go around. The training officer says that you can use his duty firearm. He brings his duty weapon into the training and shows both of you that the weapon is clear of any ammunition and is safe.

What do you do?

Course of Action: _____

_____

_____

_____

_____

_____

_____

_____

_____

_____

_____

_____

_____

_____

Scenario #96: 5 Second Ride

You are attending a Taser certification class conducted by your department. You and the instructor do not get along well. Despite this you volunteer to take the "5 Second Ride." The instructor Tasers you and two safety officers by your side guide you to the ground so that you do not get hurt. After the 5 seconds you begin to get up when the instructor yells, *"Non-compliant subject"* and he Tasers you for another 5 seconds. During the second implementation of the Taser your face slams into the ground causing minor facial bruising.

What do you do?

Course of Action: _____

_____

_____

_____

_____

_____

_____

_____

_____

_____

_____

_____

_____

_____

_____

Scott Kirshner

Scenario #97: A Bit Tipsy

You are attending a Firearms Training Academy to become an armed probation/parole officer. This is an intense 40 hour class where safety is stressed at all times. On the morning of your third day of training one of the instructors is talking about how he went out partying last night and drank a bit too much. This is the same officer who is facilitating your range training this morning. You and some of your fellow officers have noted that he still appears to be under the influence of alcohol.

What do you do?

Course of Action: _____

_____

_____

_____

_____

_____

_____

_____

_____

_____

_____

_____

_____

_____

_____

Scenario #98: Disruptive Officer in Training

During a mandatory officer safety training class a fellow officer is not listening and is being disruptive in the class. The trainer and this officer are good friends. Everyone is surprised that the instructor has not told this officer to stop being disruptive during class. This is a required safety refresher with a test at the end of class. All officers are required to pass the test. Some of the officers have told the disruptive officer to chill out but to no avail.

What do you do?

Course of Action: _____

_____

_____

_____

_____

_____

_____

_____

_____

_____

_____

_____

_____

_____

<u>Scenario #99: Lack of Safety Equipment</u>

During a force-on-force training class officers are placed in scenarios where they must engage a violent subject with a gun. During this class SIMUNITION rounds are being used. There is not enough safety equipment and you were not provided throat protection.

What do you do?

Course of Action: _____

_____

_____

_____

_____

_____

_____

_____

_____

_____

_____

_____

_____

_____

_____

_____

Scenario #100: Officer Down

You are a participant in a force-on-force training class. During a scenario that you and a group of officer are observing you hear what appears to be a gunshot from a firearm. All of a sudden the officer in the scenario falls to the ground and is bleeding profusely from his head.

What do you do?

Course of Action: _____

_____

_____

_____

_____

_____

_____

_____

_____

_____

_____

_____

_____

_____

_____

_____

_____

_____

_____

Final Thoughts

Use of force incidents may not be common within the profession of community corrections yet this is not an excuse to avoid training. When a use of force incident does occur it can have deadly consequences. Even when the outcome is not deadly there is also the possibility of serious and lifelong injury occurring. Having the ability to effectively and appropriately respond to violence is an absolutely necessary skillset for officers. You must have the ability to respond to violence appropriately, in a timely manner and under stress. The only way to achieve this ability is through training that is realistic and ongoing.

The training scenarios provided in this book can be used in a multitude of ways such as:

- Reviewed individually

- Reviewed in a group setting

- Utilized to role-play in physical training

- Converted into force-on-force training scenarios

  [NOTE: *When utilized in force-on-force training these scenarios will need to be significantly modified to adhere to all safety rules. This should only be done by an authorized trainer who has the training and experience facilitating force-on-force training.*]

Using the same training scenario in different formats will provide you new appreciation between the difference of "discussing" a scenario verse "role-playing" the scenario in a scenario based training environment. The difference can be as profound as explaining what it is like to swim as opposed to actually swimming in a pool. There is a world of difference between the two. It is also important to realize how seemingly slight modifications to a scenario can significantly impact the response of the officer. When scenarios are reviewed in a group setting you will have a better understanding of how different officers may respond differently to the same situation. This information can be insightful and very informative. It provides opportunity to discuss "why" one officer will choose one force option while another officer will choose a different force option. These discussions can provide a perspective that you have not previously thought about in terms of use of force situations.

When reviewing and discussing scenarios in a group format do not rush the process. It is vital to allow enough time for each scenario so that officers have time to think about and discuss their thought process. It is not necessarily about how many scenarios you can get through but more about discussing each scenario comprehensively. The quality of the discussion is much more important than the quantity of scenarios that you review. Over time you can get through the scenarios that you want to discuss.

When possible avoidance and retreat are the best options. Not having to resort to the utilization of force is the best case scenario. In reality, you do not always get to make that decision. The offender, subject or circumstances may not allow for avoidance or retreat in which case you have no other choice but to protect yourself or others. This can end up being the "*worst case scenario*" and your training must always be geared toward resolving this type of violence. If it does not then your training is failing you. When faced with life-threatening violence you must: **Win – Survive – Prevail**. There is no alternative. It is easy to want to ignore this reality but it is not realistic.

As I often say:

Hope is not a survival strategy.

Ignorance is not bliss; it is ignorant.

Train hard.

When you have trained and prepared for the worst case scenario you will also be adequately trained to resolve the best case scenario. Departments and officers can come up with many reasons, justifications and rationalizations why training is not a priority. One of the most common statements I hear is: "*Nothing has ever happened in the past.*" Do not fall for such rhetoric or try to convince yourself that such beliefs are true. Because, if you find yourself the victim of violence in the course of performing your job duties it is you that will suffer the consequences for not training or not being properly trained. At this point all previous rationalizations and justifications will take on a whole new meaning.

About The Author

Scott Kirshner, M.Ed., has held many positions within the criminal justice system and has extensive experience in officer safety and survival. He has been a Parole Administrator, Supervisory Probation Officer, Probation Officer, and a Correctional Officer. Throughout his career he was an officer survival instructor and was integral in the development and implementation of officer safety curriculum. He served as a Certified Firearms Instructor, Lead Defensive Tactics instructor, and has a black belt in three martial arts. He taught classes on: Use of Force, Tactical Mindset, Applied Defensive Tactics, Low-light Shooting, Force-on-Force Scenario Based Training, Judgmental Shooting, Verbal De-escalation, Safety Policies, OC Spray, Expandable Baton, and other related courses. He has consulted and provided training for probation and court departments on staff safety.

Mr. Kirshner has worked with numerous municipal, county, state, and federal law enforcement agencies relating to probation and parole. He has trained with many government and private agencies on topics to include: officer survival, active shooter intervention, force-on-force training, shoot house instructor, terrorism, weapons of mass destruction, building searches, school violence, workplace violence, flashbang operator, tactical scouting, tactical first aid and others.

<u>Books by Scott Kirshner</u>

- **Officer Survival for Probation and Parole Officers**

- **Surviving Violent Encounters: Win – Survive – Prevail**

- **Goal Setting for Law Enforcement Officers: Be a Survival Oriented Officer**

You can also "Like" his Facebook page:

Officer Survival for Probation and Parole Officers

www.Facebook.com/CommitToWin

<u>References</u>

[i] http://www.justice.gov/sites/default/files/opa/press-releases/attachments/2015/03/04/doj_report_on_shooting_of_michael_brown_1.pdf

[ii] Ibid

[iii] Ibid

[iv] Ibid

[v] Ibid

[vi] http://www.justice.gov/sites/default/files/opa/press-releases/attachments/2015/03/04/ferguson_police_department_report.pdf

32481770R00122